ED SEA / INDIAN OCEAN

pt
1 ...hag Rock
2 ...ha'b Abu Nuhas
3 ...histegorm
4 ...as Zatar
5 Ras Muhammad
6 Shark Reef
7 Jolanda Reef
8 Gordon Reef
9 Jackson Reef
10 Panorama Reef
11 Salem Express
12 Elphinstone Reef
13 Port Ghalib
14 Brothers Islands
15 Marsa Alam
16 Daedalus Reef
17 Sha'b Samadai

Sudan
1 Blue Belt
2 Sanganeb Reef
3 Sha'b Rumi
4 Umbria

Oman
1 Kachalu
2 Mushroom
3 Doc's Wall
4 Coral Garden
5 Police

Seychelles
1 Shark Bank
2 L'Ilot
3 Ennerdale
4 Brissare Rocks
5 Whale Rocks
6 Desroches
7 The Boulders
8 Aldabra Group

Mozambique
1 Two-Mile Reef
2 Cabo San Sebastian
3 The Office
4 Pandaine Express
5 Manta Reef
6 Pinnacles

Maldives
1 Gaafaru Reef
2 Bodu Hithi Thila
3 Rasfari
4 Girifushi Thila
5 Lankanfinolhu
6 Maaya Thila
7 Hukurvelhi Faru
8 Filitheyo
9 Nilandhoo
10 Dharaboodoo

0   500 miles
0   500   1000 kilometres

The World's Great
Dive Sites

The World's Great
Dive Sites

Lawson Wood

JOHN BEAUFOY PUBLISHING

*Above, left to right:
Anemonefish can
be found in most
species of anemone;
Whale Shark
(Rhincodon typus),
the largest fish
in the world; sea
slugs are incredibly
diverse in shape,
size and colour.*

5

Introduction

Tropical Diving at its Best

In compiling this selection of the best tropical diving in the world, I have inevitably made a personal choice and so I will have omitted some sites that others would have included. The intention behind the book is to highlight the pick of the world's tropical destinations so that readers will be encouraged to explore them and to have fun doing so. The selection is based on water temperature: some tropical destinations are not here because of their cooler, more temperate waters.

The locations featured in this book encompass all types of dive and should suit all divers of mixed ability. The dives include a variety of features to appeal to those with special enthusiasms, such as marine biology, underwater photography, love of historic shipwrecks or even modern ships sunk as tourism attractions. I know that other great dives can be found in the immediate vicinity of those mentioned, but what we have here

Dive sites map key

◩ Dive site
● City, town or village
■ Cenote
— Main road
-■- International boundary
〜 Water feature

provides a taste of what is available and what I have enjoyed especially. In fact, every destination chosen for this book could easily have an illustrated book specifically devoted just to it – indeed many already have.

I suggest that it isn't really helpful to compare diving conditions or the quality of marine life between oceans, countries or indeed individual dive sites. Each location has its own character and offers a wide variety of dives. Many of the destinations featured are fantastic places to learn to dive, and for many divers these sites will represent their first experience of tropical underwater habitats. Each location also offers superb snorkelling and for many travellers this will be their introduction to the underwater world. In fact, many encounters with some of the world's largest creatures are only achievable by snorkelling. With over 270 dive sites, there is a huge range of exciting underwater places to explore and enjoy.

Right: Our coral reefs can be enjoyed by everyone.

Red Sea

The Red Sea is the most northerly of the true coral reefs in the world and certainly the closest coral reef to Europe. As a result, it hosts more visiting scuba divers than any other place on the planet. It is 2,250 km (1,400 miles) long with its widest part at Massawa in Eritrea at 355 km (220 miles) while its narrowest is only 26 km (16 miles) at the Bab el Mandeb Strait in Yemen. Over 40 per cent of the Red Sea is less than 100 m (330 ft) deep while the deepest section is a narrow trough over 2,500 m (8,200 ft) deep.

The Red Sea is an offshoot of the Indian Ocean. As it extends northwards it splits into two at Ras Muhammad (the most southerly tip of the Sinai Peninsula). The left fork, the Gulf of Suez, is part of one of the world's most important trade routes while the right fork, the Gulf of Aqaba, passes up through the Straits of Tiran all the way to the Israeli tourist city of Eilat and Aqaba in Jordan.

Above: Whip Coral Blennies (Bryanopsis loki) are a common sight on many reefs.

Left: Buddy, Reeta Tunney, swims with a school of goatfish on a Red Sea reef.

Egypt

Because this is essentially an enclosed sea, there is minimal tidal range and few strong currents except around exposed reefs and headlands such as Ras Muhammad, Tiran Islands, Elphinstone, Daedalus and the Brothers Islands. Local currents through Sha'b Ali and the *Thistlegorm* wreck can be quite punishing, but overall the diving is fairly easy and suitable for all levels of diver.

Reef walls can drop from just 1 m (3 ft) to depths of many hundreds of metres, making them absolutely ideal for snorkelling, spectacular wall dives then also become accessible for novice divers and perfect for more experienced divers who may wish to do additional safety stops up the edge of the reef.

The Straits of Tiran are one of the world's busiest waterways and right in the middle of the straits are four isolated reefs which are legendary for the high quality of corals, fish life and wrecks. They are Gordon Reef, Thomas Reef, Woodhouse Reef and Jackson Reef. These reefs are all accessible by the day-dive boats out of Na'ama Bay, but live-aboards all have additional tenders to drop off and pick up divers here, so you will have the chance to dive all the way around each of the reefs.

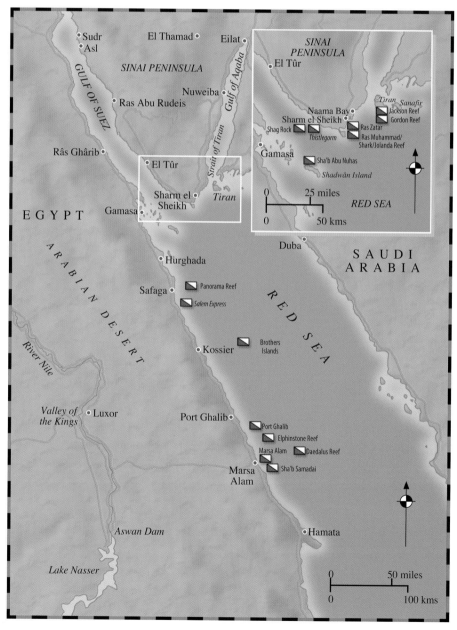

TRAVEL ADVISORY EGYPTIAN RED SEA

Climate: The Red Sea has no rain to speak of and the only vagaries in the weather are the cooler winds from the northeast from November to March and the southwesterly winds from the Sahara for the rest of the time. Those diving from live-aboards will always experience a cooler breeze in the evenings, at other times with high temperatures and no humidity you are not so aware of the heat.

When to go: Any time all year round. This enclosed sea is one of the few locations which is great at any time. There are larger concentrations of fish off Ras Muhammad in June to September.

Getting there: There are direct flights into Sharm el Sheikh, Hurghada and Marsa Alam from all the European international airports, with flight times around five hours.

Water temperature: Averages 24–26° C (75–79° F) throughout the year but can drop to 20° C (68° F) in the north with visibility averaging around 25 m (80 ft).

Quality of marine life: For such a geographical position, this most northerly coral reef is superb with excellent corals, masses of colour and fish life. You are guaranteed great encounters with turtles, massive schools of fish and above average diving conditions. Night diving is always excellent with high concentrations of invertebrates.

Depth of dives: Averages around 30 m (100 ft) but most dives on the outer reef walls will be much deeper; however, you should spend just as much time in the shallows as there is more colour, more time and more marine life.

Dive practicalities: The diving is fairly easy overall, but because the water temperatures are fairly low, you will need a full suit, particularly in the winter months when the cooler surface temperatures can be particularly cutting when returning to the dive boat by zodiac. Dehydration is another factor to be considered as the dry heat evaporates any sweat, so you must drink lots of water.

Jackson Reef

Jackson Reef is oval in shape and has the remains of the MV *Lara* on her northwestern point. The *Lara* was run aground as part of an insurance scam in 1983. Now only small parts of her rusted superstructure remain, all the rest of the ship has been pounded into pieces and has dropped down the near vertical coral wall. She is deemed only accessible to technical divers.

As the currents flow south around Jackson Reef, there is a pocket of calm, still water around the southern tip and this can be dived at any time of the day. This point has a more steeply sloping wall as opposed to the vertical wall structure to the west, making it a nice easy dive to view turtles, jacks, Yellow Goatfish (*Mulloidichthys martinicus*) and plenty of colourful soft and hard corals, sea whips and black coral trees. There are small caverns where 'sleeping' Whitetip Reef Sharks (*Triaenodon obesus*) can be found and the wall has some huge gorgonian sea fans which play host to Longnose Hawkfish (*Oxycirrhites typus*), various wrasse and schools of glassfish.

Previous page: Clockwise from top left: Masked Butterflyfish (Chaetodon semilarvatus) are endemic to the Red Sea; the Red Sea reefs are a photographer's delight; dive boats get ready to leave Marsa Alam; schools of barracuda are a common site off most exposed headlands.

Below: Probably the most predominant fish type that you will recognize in the Red Sea are anthias. The reef fringe has millions of these colourful fish all darting out into the current to feed, then returning to the safety of the reef.

Gordon Reef

Above: *Crocodilefish (Papilloculiceps longiceps) are a relative of the scorpionfish and prefer coral rubble or sandy areas where they lie in wait for their prey.*

Gordon Reef to the south is roughly circular in shape with the remains of at least two wrecks on her, the *Loullia* which ran aground in 1981 and an unnamed vessel which was carrying spools of wire which lies to the west of the reef. This wreckage is almost completely encrusted by marine growth now and little can be found of her, but most of the remains of the *Loullia* are still high and dry on the reef, though rapidly collapsing. The southeast corner of Gordon Reef is where dive boats moor up for the day and night, as the shallow sand slope starts at around 5 m (17 ft) and drops steadily to over 25 m (80 ft) before going over the wall. There are numerous small coral heads all over this site allowing you plenty of time to explore the area. The shallower reef section is sheltered and the snorkelling is superb around the fringes. Coral Grouper (*Cephalopholis miniata*), Emperor Angelfish (*Pomacanthus imperator*), Picasso Triggerfish (*Rhinecanthus aculeatus*) and Crocodilefish (*Papilloculiceps longiceps*) are common here. Be careful of the Titan Triggerfish (*Balistoides viridescens*) which are very territorial and will attack if you get too close to their nesting area amidst the coral rubble.

Above: *Emperor Angelfish (Pomacanthus imperator) are usually seen in lifelong mating pairs on many Red Sea reefs. Although shy in nature, they are always a delight to observe.*

Ras Zatar

Ras Zatar is the exposed headland at the southernmost point of a large bay called Marsa Bureika. A very steep sloping and vertical wall in many parts, particularly as you approach the corner to the bay, it is deeply indented by large fissures which cut into the headland. Most divers just swim off the reef, travelling north until they reach the first of the fissures. It is here that there are numerous caves and caverns all filled with thousands of Glassy Sweepers (*Pempheris schomburgkii*), squirrelfish, soldierfish, lionfish and grouper.

Rarely dived as there are no permanent moorings on the site, the best time to dive the reef is in the morning when the sun simply lights up the beautiful soft corals which smother the wall.

Below: Huge pale-coloured gorgonian sea fans stretch out to catch any nutrients from the mild current here.

Ras Muhammad

Ras Muhammad is the southernmost point of the Sinai Peninsula and is renowned as one of the top dives on the planet. Now a marine nature reserve, the vertical fringing coral wall drops from the surface to well beyond the limits of any recreational and technical diving. Its location exposes it to the tidal currents which pass from the Gulf of Aqaba and the Gulf of Suez. These tidal confluences also result in very high concentrations of fish life, as well as very healthy and well replenished hard and soft corals. Three small coral heads are joined to the shore via a coral rubble and sandy saddle and the reefs form the outer fringe before they drop precipitously into the depths. These are known as **Shark Reef** to the northeast, **Jolanda Reef** to the southwest and the much smaller Small Reef or The Tower beyond the Jolanda.

Shark Reef is the outer edge. Currents can be quite strong as they sweep around the outer wall, but most dive boats will drop you into the water just before the reef wall and allow the current to take you around the reef in a rather easy drift dive to swim among the simply massive schools of barracuda, Unicorn Surgeonfish (*Naso unicornis*), emperorfish, batfish and jacks. Sharks do come close into the reef, but they are generally in depths below 36 m (120 ft). The colours of the soft corals on this wall are stunning and you will marvel as you drift past at a leisurely pace surrounded by anthias. As you sweep around to the southwest, the last part of the vertical wall has numerous large caverns indented into the reef

Above: The wall at Ras Muhammad leading towards Shark Reef is vertical and undercut in many areas. This is typical of many of the Red Sea reefs.

where you can hide away from the current to concentrate on fish watching and photography. From here you drop down onto a wide sand and coral rubble slope which is dotted with coral heads, under which you will find large moray eels, scorpionfish and stonefish.

The current gradually takes you over this area to the next section of large isolated reef. This has a mini-wall dropping from the surface to 9 m (30 ft) before sloping steeply away to plunge over the wall at around 40 m (130 ft). Large indentations in the wall are filled with Glassy Sweepers and hatchetfish, with their attendant lionfish, scorpionfish, soldierfish and Bigeye Snapper (*Lutjanus lutjanus*). As the current sweeps you around the last corner at the end of your dive, you will start to spot the cargo remains of the *Jolanda*.

The *Jolanda* was on her way from Piraeus to Aqaba with a cargo including several containers of general goods. Caught in a storm in April 1980 she ran aground on the outer reef. Her anchors were pulled and steel hawsers lashed her to a small round pinnacle next to the shore, but she keeled over in four days and her cargo spilled out onto the coral rubble saddle. A superb dive site for a number of years, her weight dangling out into the blue finally pulled her anchors free, and she snapped the hawsers and plunged down the wall to rest in depths from 145–200 m (475–650 ft).

Sha'b Abu Nuhas

Sha'b Abu Nuhas is quite an exposed triangular-shaped reef with little shelter lying very close to the main sea lanes for shipping. Abu Nuhas has some superb shipwrecks on her northern reef edge. To the west is the *Giannis D*, a cargo ship filled with sawn softwood that ran aground on 19 April 1983. I was the first to dive her accommodation, rear holds and engine rooms, when she was still only partly submerged. The ship is now well broken up with her stern section largely intact and incredibly photogenic. In only 18 m (60 ft) of water, her engine room is penetrable and divers enjoy the swim around her funnel and aft railings.

Two years later, at the northeast corner of Abu Nuhas, I was in a group of divers who discovered the remains of another shipwreck, which I later identified, with the help of P&O's archivist, as the P&O ship *Carnatic*, lost in 1869 taking with her five passengers and 26 crew. The ship is completely open in aspect with her deck timbers having rotted away, leaving all of her decks accessible. This is an absolutely superb dive through a fabulously rich and colourful wreck.

Further to the east of the *Carnatic* and now also completely underwater, there are another two shipwrecks, the *Kimon M* which sank in 1978 and the *Chrisoula K* which ran aground in August 1981. The *Chrisoula K* was carrying a cargo of travertine floor tiles when she ran onto the corner of the reef at full speed resulting in her total loss. She lies fairly upright and her holds are open allowing easy access through her. This corner of the reef is quite exposed and can be fairly rough making diving conditions difficult.

Above: A diver explores the interior of the *Carnatic on Abu Nuhas reef.*

Opposite: Shipwrecks soon become encrusted with soft and hard corals and become part of the existing reef.

Above: *The SS Kingston ran aground in 1881 and is a favourite dive for many photographers as her stern decks are easily penetrated.*

Left: *The distinctive stern of the Thistlegorm with her circular gun platform and aft companionway are rarely visited, as most divers spend their time in the forward holds.*

Shag Rock

Further up the Gulf of Suez past Sha'b Ali is another triangular-shaped reef called **Shag Rock**. The identity of a wreck here was unknown for many years and she was misnamed many times until she was found to be the steamship *Kingston*, which ran aground in 1881 carrying a cargo of coal. The ship stretches out into the Gulf where the fringing reef has completely overgrown all of its shallower portions. It is only when you swim from the stern that you can appreciate the full majesty of this ship as she sits on the seabed, virtually intact. A pod of wild dolphins are found in this area as are large numbers of snapper and fusiliers as well as Napoleon Wrasse (*Cheilinus undulatus*) and tons of anthias. The hard corals on the reef edge are superb.

The SS *Thistlegorm*

Perhaps the jewel in the crown for many divers is the **SS *Thistlegorm*** lost to German Heinkel bombers on 6 October 1941 in the protected water of Sha'b Ali in the southeastern stretch of the Gulf of Suez. She was absolutely stuffed full with all of the machinery of war, including railway locomotives, motorbikes and trucks. Nine sailors lost their lives that night.

The *Thistlegorm* is one of those dives that just has to be done time and again. Her forward holds are completely open and you can swim around her cargo of motorbikes and trucks. The bridge and stern are largely intact and her gun is still prominent on the circular mounting platform. Due to the surrounding shallow waters of the reef, the visibility is generally around 12–15 m (30–40 ft). The fact that she is very popular also results in reduced visibility in the holds and deck area. The best option for diving the wreck is from a live-aboard dive boat which can moor directly onto the ship, allowing you the chance to dive her at night and again at first light before the madding crowd arrives.

Above: The interior holds of the SS Thistlegorm are filled with all the machinery of war. There are motorbikes, trucks, jeeps, aircraft parts, guns, ammunition and so much more to see that you need to dive it many times.

Brother Islands

These two small islands sit well out into the main tidal stream that is constantly fed and replenished by the plankton-rich waters. There is very little dive-boat traffic to the two islands and special permits are required to ensure that all boats and divers observe a strict conservation code. Consequently the reefs are pristine. **Big Brother** has a British-built lighthouse about half way along the barren island and this is where the dive boats moor up, running divers to the outer reef walls by zodiac. At the northern tip of Big Brother is a superbly scenic shipwreck called the *Numidia* which ran aground in July 1901 and trails into

Above: Big Brother Island is on many divers' wish list as it has pristine vertical coral walls and two superb shipwrecks covered in marine life.

the depths from the surface to over 80 m (260 ft). Surrounded by fish and in super-clear water, it is very easy to overstay your welcome at depth and so extra care should be taken.

Further to the south on **Little Brother**, a long spur of limestone drops down into the depths and thresher sharks tend to congregate here at the confluence of the currents. This dive is only for experienced divers and there have been instances of divers being swept away in the current, so great care is required.

The *Salem Express*

The *Salem Express* was a ferry that worked between Jeddah in Saudi Arabia and Safaga in Egypt. Reportedly overloaded with vehicles and passengers in December 1991, returning from a pilgrimage to Mecca, she encountered a massive storm and ran at full speed onto Hyndman Reef, causing her massive bow door to open. The sea rushed in with such force that she rolled over and sank in under ten minutes. One of the worst tragedies ever recorded in the Red Sea, the true numbers of passengers lost is unknown, though thankfully 180 passengers and crew did survive. The massive loss of life colours your feelings on this dive and the atmosphere can be quite eerie.

You are able to swim all the way through the cavernous vehicle deck, but seeing the possessions of those lost is very poignant and many divers prefer to stay on the outside. For those who do dive the ship, please respect the loss of life and do not touch the possessions of those who died.

Panorama Reef

Panorama Reef near Safaga is usually dived after a visit to the *Salem Express*. Similar in profile to Jackson Reef, live-aboard dive boats are able to moor up in safety allowing you the chance to enjoy late afternoon dives and a night dive. This vertical wall can be approached in many ways. The western edge of the wall is better for coral growth, while the outer (eastern) reef is exposed and often has strong current. When conditions are optimum, the dive is excellent with very good encounters with turtle, large Napoleon Wrasse, parrotfish and multitudes of anthias.

Some areas are vertical, others have steep slopes; other parts have small plateaus of large acropora table corals. You can find Blue-spotted Stingrays (*Taeniura lymna*), large moray eels, and an anemone garden with literally hundreds of clownfish and damselfish which is certainly on a par with that at Ras Muhammad.

Below: The Salem Express was lost in a sudden storm in December 1991 with a massive loss of life. Although diving on her is still controversial, the dive is relatively easy to suit all levels of diver experience.

Marsa Alam

Marsa Alam is the embarkation point for the outer reefs of Sha'b Samadai (Dolphin Reef), Elphinstone and Daedalus Reefs. Principally, the diving for the shore sites is done from the newly constructed town of **Port Ghalib** where most of the resorts are located.

With a backdrop of wonderful Egyptian mountains receding into the hazy distance, the entire shoreline is fringed with a hard coral reef which drops around 25 m (80 ft) on average, before shelving steeply into the depths. For the most part the fringing reef is fairly featureless until you come to a *marsa* or bay. These *marsas* have been carved out over aeons of time by underground freshwater streams. Corals obviously cannot live in such reduced salinity, so gradually as a result of flood water and scouring by the weather, all of the *marsas* have superb coral structures to north and south and wide sandy seagrass beds in the centre.

Below: The marsas or bays between Port Ghalib and Marsa Alam have very good fringing corals as well as established seagrass beds – a favourite food for Green Turtles (Chelonia mydas).

Sha'b Samadai

Sha'b Samadai or Dolphin Reef is always visited with a Marine Park ranger
on board, as this protected, horseshoe-shaped reef has a resident population
of Spinner Dolphins (*Stenella longirostris*). Even if they aren't in evidence, the
coral heads to the northwest of the reef are some of the best on the entire coast.
With an average depth of only 12–25 m (40–70 ft) the visibility is so good that
you can clearly see each of the narrow, vertical coral heads making navigation
simple and the diving exceptional. The largest of the reefs has a massive
open cavern system which is easily negotiable in only 6 m (20 ft) of water
with numerous exits and open shafts of light everywhere. Large sweetlips and
emperorfish inhabit this reef and all are very friendly. This is a great dive with
vertical walls covered in soft and hard corals, schools of anthias and sometimes
even a Whitetip Reef Shark or nurse sharks, not to mention the turtles. The
sandy gullies between the coral heads have a number of large anemones and
anemonefish and the small patches of seagrass host seahorses, Robust Ghost
Pipefish (*Solenostomus cyanopterus*), frogfish and sea moths. It is astonishing that
such a wide variety of rare species could be found in such a small area.

*Above: Large family groups of Spinner
Dolphins can be found at Sha'b Samadai
and Sha'b Sataya further to the south near
the Fury Shoals.*

Elphinstone Reef

The travel time of 2½ hours from either Port Ghalib or Marsa Alam to **Elphinstone Reef** is well worth the effort. This long finger reef reaches to just below the surface and so there is usually a surface surge, swell and current. Divers are briefed meticulously on how to negotiate the reef. There are vertical reef walls and large schools of jacks, spadefish, tuna, mackerel and barracuda. The shallower sections of the reef, while disturbed by the oceanic swell, have superb shoals of snapper, Racoon Butterflyfish (*Chaetodon lunula*) and pufferfish.

Opposite: The eastern wall of Elphinstone Reef is vertical in nature and very reminiscent of the Brother Islands' walls to the north. Best dived in the morning to catch the best light, there are brilliant soft corals, huge pale sea fans and a multitude of colourful reef fish.

Daedalus Reef

Daedalus Reef is remote – around 4½ hours by boat. This small, isolated reef is a dedicated marine park almost halfway to Saudi Arabia and is 450 m (1,500 ft) long and 100 m (330 ft) wide. Few dive boats make the journey meaning the fringing reef here is in a better condition than any other dive site in the Red Sea.

Like the Brothers, strong currents run from north to south and high winds tend to whip up the surface waters making diving conditions challenging, but the underwater scenery is well worth the effort. Bigger fish such as hammerhead sharks, barracuda and even sailfish and huge tuna tend to hang out around the eddies of the converging currents at the southern tip of the reef plateau. Due to the alignment of the reef, it is better to dive the eastern wall in the morning and the western wall in the afternoon. Both walls are covered in superb gorgonian sea fans, sea whips and thickly overgrown with soft corals, particularly deep purple ones. Visibility is generally over 30 m (100 ft) making it easy to go deep without realizing it, particularly when you are chasing big fish to photograph.

Above: Large table corals (Acropora spp.) over 2 m (6½ ft) across offer shelter to Masked Butterflyfish, grouper and delicate small sponges and ascidians.

Sudan

The Sudan is the largest country in Africa with over 300 different ethnic groups and shares its borders with Eritrea, Kenya, Ethiopia, Libya, Egypt, Chad, Central African Republic, Uganda and the Congo. Offshore is the deepest area of the Red Sea at over 2,500 m (8,200 ft) deep alongside some of the most beautiful coral reefs in the Red Sea. The Sudan is one of the more difficult places to dive, principally from a political point of view as safety, of course, always has to come first. The diving done in the Sudanese Red Sea is only done by live-aboard dive boat usually embarking from Safaga, Marsa Alam or even Hurghada. From the reefs which border the southern shore of Egypt there are a number of marine protected areas including the fringing and barrier reefs of Gebel Elba in the north; and Sanganeb, Suakin and the Dahlak Archipelago (off Ethiopia) in the central and southern regions.

While there are fewer tropical fish species found here than in other similar extremities of the Indo-Pacific fisheries zone, almost 30 per cent of these are endemic to the Red Sea and testimony to her isolation over the millennia. Considering how new (in relative terms) the Red Sea is to the age of the continental masses that have shaped our planet, this number of new fish species, specific to the region, is quite remarkable, as is the density of species which can cover every available space.

Many divers extol the virtues of the southern Sudan and quite rightly so, as the reefs are the least dived in the entire region. Her marine life is more prolific and with less human intrusion (such as resorts and hotel coastal developments); there is more species diversity and there are better chances of encounters with larger species, such as hammerhead sharks, Manta Rays (*Manta birostris*) and even species of cetacean and Dugongs (*Dugong dugon*).

Opposite: Clockwise from top left: Citron Gobies (Gobiodon citrinus) resemble anemonefish but live on table corals instead; divers take a 'giant stride' entry off the rear of a Red Sea live-aboard dive boat; the long pier and reef edge at Daeadalus Reef; large schools of glassy sweepers (Pempheris schomburgki) are found in many caves and shallow caverns.

TRAVEL ADVISORY SUDANESE RED SEA

Climate: The Red Sea has no rain to speak of and the only vagaries in the weather are the cooler winds from the northeast from November to March and the southwesterly winds from the Sahara for the rest of the time. Those diving from live-aboards will always experience a cooler breeze in the evenings, at other times with high temperatures and no humidity you are not so aware of the heat.

When to go: Any time all year round. This enclosed sea is one of the few locations which is great at any time. There are larger concentrations of fish off Sanganeb where you can also expect good shark sightings.

Getting there: There are direct flights into Sharm el Sheikh, Hurghada, Marsa Alam and Safaga, but virtually all of the live-aboard diving here is on boats that travel down from Egypt.

Water temperature: Averages 24–26° C (75–79° F) throughout the year but can drop to 24° C (75° F) in the south with visibility averaging around 30 m (100 ft).

Quality of marine life: There are more interesting and more varied species as you move further south and a better chance for large pelagics, such as hammerheads and Grey Reef Sharks.

Depth of dives: Averages around 30 m (100 ft) but most dives on the outer reef walls will be much deeper; however, you should spend just as much time in the shallows as there is more colour, more time and more marine life.

Dive practicalities: The diving is fairly easy overall, but you will be spending the entire time on a boat. Diving is suited to all levels as many of the best wrecks are in very shallow water.

The *Blue Belt*

The *Blue Belt* was a former Saudi Arabian cargo vessel which struck Sha'b Suedi Reef 80 km (50 miles) north of Port Sudan in December 1977 carrying a cargo of 181 cars and six trucks. Trying to get through a narrow gap in the reef, she struck it and started to list. Salvage operators removed much of the cargo in an unsuccessful attempt to refloat the ship, hence it is now scattered all around the ship which has become known as the 'Toyota Wreck'. The scale of the shipwreck is massive at 103 m (337 ft) and there are fairly good low-lying soft and hard corals which have totally encrusted all of the cars and trucks. The ship is penetrable and there is a nice swim through at the bows. Lying in depths of 10–36 m (30–118 ft), and upside down at an angle of around 30° on the reef slope, the hull is fairly featureless and rather dull – the coral reef up Fasima Suedi at the end of the dive is generally better than the wreck itself.

Sha'b Rumi

Sha'b Rumi is one of the more famous reefs off the Sudan, not least because it was the location for Jacques-Yves Cousteau's *Conshelf II* or *Precontinent II* experiment in underwater living. Following the success of his first experiment off Marseilles in France, a year later in 1963 he chose the Sudan as the base for housing an eight-man team to remain underwater for a month to conduct experiments and scientific study. In a depth of 12 m (40 ft), 35 km (22 miles) from Port Sudan, a dome 'house' with five rooms and all 'mod cons' was placed underwater. A garage nearby held a small bathysphere for descending over 300 m (1,000 ft) off the continental shelf; an additional submersible cabin was attached as well as some deepwater shark cages at around 50 m (165 ft). A further 25 divers undertook the necessary maintenance and supply for those in the watertight spheres.

Above: Spanish Dancer nudibranchs (Hexabranchia sanguineus) are usually only found during night dives. At around 30 cm (12 in) long, they are the largest nudibranchs or seaslugs found in the Red Sea.

Now 50 years later, the buildings are still in remarkably good condition and covered in superb soft and hard corals. The area abounds with fish and the shark cage at around 30 m (100 ft) is covered with good soft corals and sponges. The nearby reef is also excellent and well worth exploring as you ascend into shallower water. Even after all this time, the success of the underwater experiment is still very evident and everyone who dives it can share that history.

The south side of the Sha'b Rumi plateau is well known for the possibility of sightings of Grey Reef Sharks (*Carcharhinus amblyrhynchos*) which are found regularly on the plateau. Interestingly there are also species of fish found in the south which never quite get as far as Ras Muhammad, such as Bumphead Parrotfish (*Bolbometopon muricatum*) and snapper more commonly found in the Indian Ocean.

Below: This underwater structure, placed by Jacques-Yves Cousteau as part of an underwater living experiment, is still fairly intact after over 50 years underwater.

Sanganeb Reef

Sanganeb Reef is an isolated offshore island. Rising majestically from the depths, the vertical reef walls are covered with a profusion of soft and hard corals. Large pelagics are lured here by the chance of food species and cleaner stations, and you can see both predator and prey lined up to get cleaned of parasites, all enmity forgotten (for the moment). Anthias are prevalent as are some large barracuda, jacks, trevally and surgeonfish. Although not as filled with fish life as you would expect, there are great black coral trees and gorgonian sea fans, plenty of small chromis, wrasse, numerous lionfish and coral groupers.

On the southern plateau sharks are more common and have been known to come pretty close to divers. This is principally because the sharks used to be fed here at one time and while this is no longer allowed, the sharks have long memories! There are always plenty of goatfish, batfish, barracuda, snapper, angelfish and butterflyfish and overall the reef is in excellent condition with very good quality hard and soft corals, sea fans, whips and sponges.

Below: There are several species of lionfish found in the Red Sea, the largest being the Red Lionfish (Pterois volitans) which tends to live nearby schools of Glassy Sweepers (Pempheris schomburgkii) and coral heads with damselfish.

The *Umbria*

The *Umbria* was originally built in Hamburg in 1911 and was bought by Italy to transport munitions in 1935. Early on in the war, the ship was at anchor close to shore near Port Sudan when she was impounded and searched by a British Royal Navy boarding party looking (supposedly) for contraband. The captain of the ship scuttled her while the boarding party was still on board, sinking her and her cargo of 360,000 bombs. After the war, a British bomb-disposal group looked to clear the wreck but realized that if they blew the ship up, it would take most of Port Sudan with it. Divers are obviously warned not to interfere with the bombs but much of the diving is in the shallower open areas away from the holds that have to be penetrated.

Often classed as the 'perfect' wreck dive, the *Umbria* is big enough to give you plenty to explore, small enough to dive most of it on a single dive, shallow enough to spend lots of time in some of the most photogenic parts of the ship, open enough to explore into her holds, and deep enough to ensure that the lower sections are covered with superb soft and hard corals. Tons of fish are everywhere, as well as good quality sponges, crinoids, sea squirts and clams. Cleaning stations, large anemones and clownfish, moray eels and scorpionfish are all evident, as are small schools of Glassy Sweepers, hatchetfish and fusiliers. Lying on her port side with parts of her railings at the surface and the deepest portions in only 38 m (124 ft), the 150-m (500-ft) long ship is simply stunning and divers and snorkellers can expect many hours of pleasure exploring the ship and her artefacts.

Above: This anemonefish (Amphiprion bicinctus) is endemic to the Red Sea and is very common on all of the reefs. It enjoys the company of small damselfish and various species of shrimp which also live within the anemone's tentacles.

Indian Ocean

The Indian Ocean covers 73,550,000 sq km (28,400,000 sq miles) – approximately 20 per cent of the world's water surface – making it the third largest ocean in the world. The greatest diversity of marine life on the planet is found within this zone from penguins to parrotfish and seals to seahorses. It contains several major island groups with magnificent diving opportunities.

Within this broad expanse, the Indian Ocean includes the Gulf of Aden which opens up into the Red Sea which leads into the Gulf of Aqaba and the Gulf of Suez; the Arabian Sea which leads further to the Gulf of Oman and the Arabian or Persian Gulf; the Mozambique Channel; the Andaman Sea within the Bay of Bengal; the Straits of Malacca, the busiest shipping route in the world; the waters off northern Australia to the Timor Sea and Arafura Sea; the Great Australian Bight and the Bass Straits between Australia and Tasmania.

Above: Manta Rays (Manta birostris) *are commonly found on many Maldives dive sites.*

Left: Golden Cup Corals (Tubastrea aurea) *light up the coral reefs at night when their polyps open.*

Oman

The Sultanate of Oman is highly regarded as one of the most stable and developed countries in the Arab World and covers an area of around 309,500 sq km (192,300 sq miles). Most tourists visit because of its desert scenery and the lush green oases high in the desert mountains.

Oman has over 3,165 km (1,966 miles) of coastline formed by the Arabian Sea on the southeast and the Gulf of Oman on the northeast. It is separated from the Persian Gulf at Musandam and the Strait of Hormuz. The country is bisected by the Tropic of Cancer, and is rapidly gaining in popularity with discerning scuba divers who want to experience something just a little different.

Whale Sharks (*Rhincodon typus*) are regular visitors through the straits as are large stingrays and even Manta Rays (*Manta birostris*). A few of the wrecks have large numbers of rays around them all year and Spotted Moray eels (*Gymnothorax moringa*) are so common that they are seen on every dive. Invertebrate life is extremely rich in these latitudes and divers should insist on night diving as often as possible as there is just so much colour highlighted by your torchlight.

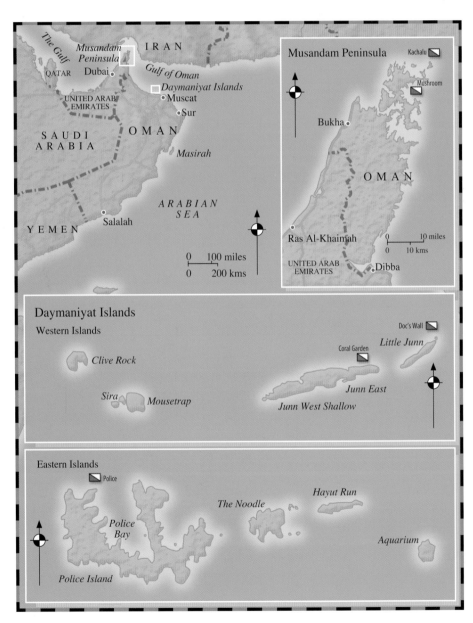

TRAVEL ADVISORY OMAN

Climate: Very hot with very little rainfall; temperatures reach around 50° C (122° F) in the hot season from May to September. Annual rainfall in Muscat averages 100 mm (4 in), falling mostly in January. Dhofar is subject to the southwest monsoon, and rainfall up to 640 mm (25 in) has been recorded in the rainy season from late June to October. The mountain areas receive most rain; some parts of the coast, particularly near the island of Masirah, sometimes receive no rain at all in a year.

When to go: November through March see stable conditions and although the water is cooler and usually has a plankton bloom, this is perfect for the chances of seeing large game fish.

Getting there: Flights to Muscat are regular and international connections are available through most European 'hub' airports as well as from London and of course the regional airports in Abu Dhabi and Dubai.

Water temperature: Averages 27° C (80° F) in summer, 21° C (68° F) in winter. Visibility is entirely variable due to the tidal currents which sweep through the straits.

Quality of marine life: Corals are much smaller and 'scrubby' compared to other locations in the central Indian Ocean but they are plentiful and very colourful, with plenty of chances for encounters with oceanic species including lots of shark species, as well as lots of different moray eels on every dive.

Depth of dives: Averages around 6–25 m (20–80 ft) but a few of the offshore sites are much deeper.

Dive practicalities: Hugely influenced by the shallow sandbars and cooler waters, divers should wear full wetsuits at all times and have warm clothing available for some long boat trips to and from the outer islands.

Daymaniyat Islands

The **Daymaniyat Islands Nature Reserve** is located about 18 km (12 miles) off the coast of Barka 70 km (43 miles) west of Muscat. Its total area is 100 ha (247 acres) and it is composed of nine islands. This reserve has a rich natural heritage and is well known for its coral reefs,. The islands are home to a large number of turtles that nest and lay their eggs on the secluded empty beaches.

The Daymaniyat Islands or 'the String of Pearls' run from east to west and are easily accessed from As Sawadi by the fast, shallow-drafted, rigid hull boats that hold around eight divers each. The average depth of the dives is around 15–18 m (50–60 ft). One of the further sites is called **Police** which has large numbers of Honeycomb Moray eels (*Gymnothorax favagineus*), most of which are out in the open on the rocky, coral-encrusted pinnacles. As you proceed out towards the point, the current picks up and this is reflected in the quality and colour of the soft corals. On the island of Junn, there are several dives, each distinct, yet all of them having the same interesting selection of marine life. At the **Coral Garden** there is a real diversity of hard and soft corals, black coral trees and sea whips. The highlight was finding a Leopard Shark (*Triakis semifasciata*) resting on the sand. Fish life is very good here with large schools of batfish, barracuda and yellowtails.

Previous page: Clockwise from top left: the male Anthias is purple in colour, compared to the orange female; Whale Sharks (Rhincodon typus) are commonly seen passing through the Straits of Hormuz; small hairy spider crabs are seen on night dives amongst the purple soft corals; turtles are found everywhere as they nest on the beaches off Oman's outer islands.

Below: Glassy Sweepers (Pempheris schomburgkii) are found in recesses amidst purple soft corals, always just moving out of your arm's reach.

On **Doc's Wall**, the vertical and steeply sloping wall gradually forms into a tumble of boulders at around 25 m (80 ft) with ledges that are covered in brilliant red and purple soft corals. Anemones and their symbiotic partners Clark's Anemonefish (*Amphiprion clarkii*) abound.

Above: Honeycomb Moray eels (Gymnothorax favagineus) are common on most dives. Easily photographed, they are quite distinctive to the region.

Musandam Peninsula

Working along the Musandam Peninsula, there are around 18 different dive sites. The Strait of Hormuz and the Gulf of Oman form the boundaries of the peninsula resulting in big currents and big critters which want to swim with it and against it! Usually the dive boat is accompanied by a pod of dolphins riding the bow wave.

At a site called the **Mushroom**, I saw the usual Spotted Morays, spiny lobster, various angelfish and lionfish and lots of nudibranchs and cleaner shrimps. At **Kachalu** (or the 'Washing Machine') known widely for its unpredictably strong currents, there were schools of large jacks, Rainbow Runners (*Elagatis bipinnulata*), barracuda and snapper. With a maximum depth of 32 m (105 ft), the walls of the seamount had a curious topography, but it is difficult to stop and view as you are swept along with the fish.

Maldives

Part of the same ridge that joins Lakshadweep to the north and the Chagos Bank to the south, the Maldives cover 868 km (539 miles) of ocean from north to south. There are over 1,200 islands concentrated around some 26 major coral atolls. Each atoll may contain several resorts featuring log cabins set on stilts that stretch out into the shallow lagoons. There are three main types of diving, and the nature of the diving operation plus the skill level of the diver determines where the boats will go.

The reefs usually have several channels where the tides funnel in and out of the lagoon, and much of the drift diving takes place around the entrances to the lagoons. The outer reef walls, particularly off the more exposed western reef edges are perfect for exploring beautiful coral gardens. Some current should be expected on these dives, as well as choppy water. Last but not least are the *thila* or small coral bommies which are dotted in the channel entrances and also further into the lagoons. Usually lying around 12 m (40 ft) below the surface, these are a perfect oasis for marine life and the sites have everything concentrated in one area.

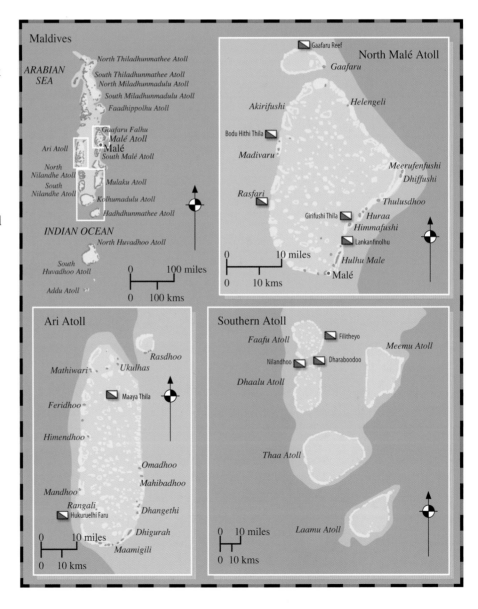

TRAVEL ADVISORY MALDIVES

Climate: 26–32° C (79–90° F) in summer and 21–24° C (70–75° F) in winter. The wet season is from May to October and the dry season is from November to April.

When to go: There are two distinct seasons in the northeastern Indian Ocean and the current pattern changes with the monsoons. Dive conditions during the dry season are at their optimum with only light winds and currents coming from the northeast between November and April.

Getting there: Flights to Hulehule Airport Island just north of Malé are numerous and easy, but usually connecting through Sri Lanka.

Water temperature: Averages 27–29° C (81–84° F) throughout the year with visibility averaging around 25 m (80 ft)

Quality of marine life: Legendary, with much of the best of what the Indian Ocean has to offer. Sightings of large pelagics are common, but most divers come for the corals, reef fish and invertebrate life.

Depth of dives: Averages around 15–30 m (50–100 ft) but most dives on the outer reefs will be much deeper, particularly if you are going big critter hunting.

Dive practicalities: Much of the diving is drift diving from small boats or live-aboards and may not be suitable for novice divers. Choose your dive resort or live-aboard dive boat well as this choice may make or break your holiday. When the stronger winds from the west are blowing, much of the diving is restricted to the lee shores where the corals are not as good nor the waters as clear.

North Malé Atoll

North Malé Atoll is huge with many little coral sand and limestone islands dotted all around the edges. Diving tends to be concentrated on the northwestern region where the open ocean diving is exemplary and the southeastern region where more resorts are located because of their proximity to the capital and airport.

Off the northern point of North Malé Atoll lies another small atoll called Gaafaru Falhu. Only reached by live-aboard dive boat, **Gaafaru Reef** is regarded as an open ocean reef and drift dive. This is a fairly easy drift dive and, depending on where you are dropped off by the dive boat, the current can carry you over at least seven obvious shipwrecks.

Bodu Hithi Thila is found between Boduhithi and Kudahithi and sits in the middle of the channel. It is only diveable during the northeast monsoon when it is completely sheltered, although the currents can still be quite strong as they exit from the inner lagoon. Here are Manta Rays (*Manta birostris*), Whale Sharks (*Rhincodon typus*), schools of batfish, numerous sharks and of course all the small filter-feeding fish which love this type of environment.

Tiny **Rasfari Island** is found further south and again is sheltered from the northeast monsoon, and so only dived in the winter months. The dive is through

Previous page: Clockwise from top left: crinoids or feather starfish (Crinoidea spp.) are found in large numbers on nearly all of the reefs; there are over 1200 islands and coral atolls in the Maldives; a typical 'stilted' Maldives resort placed over a shallow lagoon; schools of Batfish (Platax tiera) can be found at the entrances to many of the shallow lagoons.

Below: Manta Rays (Manta birostris) are typically found feeding in many lagoons particularly at night when the sea fills with planktonic life as it rises in the water column from the depths.

the channel that traverses the outer rim of the atoll. The reef plateau has an average depth of over 30 m (100 ft), but there is a little *thila* at 25 m (80 ft), while a mini-oasis of marine life including large numbers of sharks, eagle rays and barracuda is found in the strong current that sweeps around the coral head.

Shifting to the southeastern part of Malé Atoll, **Girifushi** (HP Reef) or Rainbow Reef as it is sometimes known is at the entrance of the channel which accesses the HP Reef Protected Area. The channel is absolutely stuffed full of *Dendronephya* soft corals of every colour imaginable. Due to the strong currents, this is not for novice divers as sometimes you can be pulled into deeper waters. Large pelagics and sharks are always expected here and Girifushi is regarded as one of the top dives on the atoll.

South of Paradise Island can be found **Lankanfinolhu** (Manta Point). During the southwest monsoon season, the channel and reefs here are well protected as the top of the reef is at around 12 m (40 ft). Currents are expected to be strong, but because of this the many and varied corals are in excellent order and of course there are the Manta Rays. Also feeding in the channel are large bigeyes, Oriental Sweetlips (*Plectorhinchus vittatus*) and huge wrasse. Most ledges have moray eels and cleaner shrimps and overall this site is so colourful and so full of diverse marine life that you will want to return.

Below: Colourful bluebell tunicates or sea squirts (Clavelina spp.) are only 1.5 cm (½ in) long and often appear in clusters of many hundreds of individuals.

Ari Atoll

One of the largest atolls in the country is **Ari Atoll** which is separated from the main atoll by the Alihuras Channel. On such a huge atoll, there are several Manta points, lots of sheer walls, drop-offs, caves and caverns. Hundreds of *thila* are dotted everywhere and in general, despite the tourism numbers, the reefs are healthy, the corals incredibly varied and colourful and fish life plentiful, if not excessive on some dives.

Maaya Thila Protected Area is within the lagoon in the northern part of Ari Atoll, just 3 km (2 miles) northwest of Maayaushi Resort. This dive site does get rather busy, but the site is fully protected and the conservation measures in place are effective. The *thila* is only about 30 m (100 ft) in diameter making it easy to circumnavigate on a single dive, but most time is usually spent at the point where the current is strongest. Here you will find Grey Reef Sharks (*Carcharhinus amblyrhynchos*), turtles and schools of batfish. The shallowest part of the reef is in 15 m (50 ft) and it drops down to over 40 m (130 ft), with some of the coral walls vertical and others steeply sloping.

Above: The Imperial or Yellow-faced Angelfish (Euxiphipops xanthometopon) is one of the most colourful of the angelfish found in the Indian Ocean. Although rare and usually found on their own, they are a delight to encounter.

To the southwest of the atoll is **Hukuruelhi Faru** (Madivaru) or Manta Point. Located on the southern side of Rangali Channel, Madivaru is known for its Mantas. The coral reef is shallowest at 8 m (27 ft) and drops steeply down to 30 m (100 ft). Manta cleaning stations are spread all over the reef with small wrasse and angelfish coming into open water to clean the huge Mantas of parasites. A huge basin has been carved into the reef by the waters flowing out of the lagoon and the Mantas appear to enjoy hanging out in the eddies here.

Nilandhoo

Nilandhoo consists of two atolls, Faafu in the north and Dhaalu in the south and they are located 150 km (95 miles) from Malé.

Both atolls have good dive sites and the house reef of **Filitheyo** in the north is great for finding little critters and a good variety of small corals and reef fish. At the southern point of Dhaalu are two shipwrecks, the *Liffey* which sunk in 1879 and more recently the small vessel *Utheema I* which hit the reef in 1960. Both are well broken up and any remains are now covered with soft and hard corals, fire coral, sponges and algae. With only few resorts around Nilandhoo, the dive sites are much quieter and more often than not you will find yourself on reefs which are relatively unexplored.

Above: Pseudanthias squamipinnis, *normally so lively when feeding during the day, hide amidst the hard coral recesses at night, with just their head showing.*

Dharaboodoo Point lies to the east of the house reef on Vilu Reef in northern Dhaalu. A summer season dive as it is protected by the northern atoll, it is always done on flood tides as the clear clean water sweeps you into the sheltered lagoon of the atoll. Five huge coral blocks have come away from the main reef when the undercut heads just grew too heavy on top. These now lie in the channel and are populated with every colourful fish imaginable. The house reef wall drops down to 35 m (115 ft) and is peppered with huge caves and caverns teeming with squirrelfish and soldierfish while many large grouper lurk in the shadows. Fusiliers, snapper and unicorn fish swim by in the hundreds and the entire wall is alive with basslets and chromis.

Seychelles

Consisting almost entirely of granite, the main islands of the Seychelles Archipelago have little or no fringing reef for protection. Mahé is the biggest island lying just 4° south of the Equator. Bird Island is the only true coral island in the main group, excepting of course the largest coral atoll on the planet, Aldabra, and the Amirantes Archipelago.

The Seychelles were first inhabited by humans only in the early 18th century. Like the Galapagos Islands, their oceanic isolation has allowed a vast number of rare species of animals and plants to prosper amid a lush vegetation. Many endemic birds actually thrive under the protection offered by several of the offshore and isolated islands. The Seychellois are a mix of Indians, Europeans, Asians and Africans. Today the Republic of Seychelles is an independent, non-aligned nation with a unique combination of ethnic components that has created a distinctive culture.

The underwater topography is very similar to the offshore islands of western Thailand with the 'reefs' being made of large granite boulders covered in a layer of small soft corals, cup corals and sponges. With over 900 species of fish, 100 types of shells and 50 varieties of coral, the Seychelles are an underwater photographer's dream. There is little or no current around the islands, a great variety of fish, colourful corals and a good chance of seeing large pelagics, such as marlin and Whale Sharks (*Rhincodon typus*).

Opposite page: Clockwise from top left: Christmas Tree Worms (Spirobranchus giganteus) are colourful small fan worms found growing in many hard corals; caves and caverns are fringed with black coral trees and well worth exploring; the typical granite shoreline can be very rugged and difficult to access; palm trees amidst huge granite boulders symbolize the Seychelles Islands.

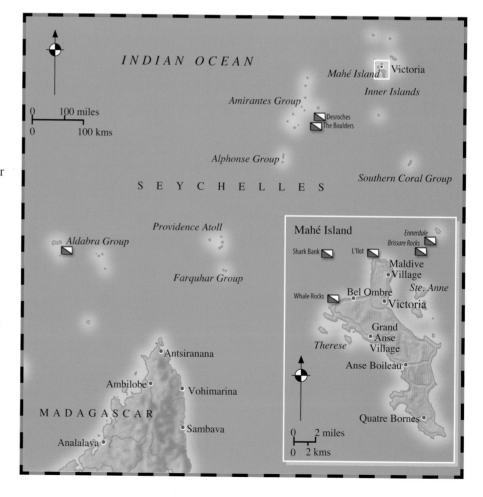

TRAVEL ADVISORY SEYCHELLES

Climate: The southeast monsoon blows from mid-May to the end of October. The highest rainfall occurs around December and January, with the hottest months being March and April. Temperatures usually in the high 20s° C (high 80s° F).

When to go: Whale Shark season is usually from August to late October and early November, so inevitably I would go then!

Getting there: Flights to Mahé international airport are serviced regularly from the UK, Singapore, Sri Lanka, South Africa, Paris and Dubai. Small internal flights will get you to the offshore islands, but for Aldabra you will require a private charter, due to security issues.

Water temperature: Averages 28° C (82° F) in summer, 26° C (79° F) in winter. Visibility is usually around 21 m (70 ft), except during the plankton bloom in the autumn when the Whale Sharks come into the shallow waters to feed.

Quality of marine life: Excellent with some 900 recorded species of fish and over 100 species of coral found here, with fish and invertebrates also prolific. However, the islands were hit very badly by La Niña and what small coral growth that was there was decimated. Thankfully it is fighting back strongly and the offshore reefs are great.

Depth of dives: Averages around 18 m (60 ft) but a few of the offshore sites are much deeper.

Dive practicalities: Some of the offshore dive sites, such as Shark Bank, the Ennerdale and Brissare Rocks are at least a 45-minute boat ride and there is often oceanic swell, so travel calm pills may be a precaution.

L'Ilot

Most of the dive sites are just a 10–20 minute boat ride from Mahé's shore. One spectacular dive is the tiny granite outcrop of **L'Ilot**. This site is bursting with marine life. *Tubastrea aurea* – the Golden Cup Coral – festoons the canyons and gulleys, gorgonian fan corals and small soft corals abound. The maximum depth is only around 12 m (40 ft) here and it is easy to negotiate the rocky outcrop on a single dive.

Slightly to the east of the rock and midway between L'Ilot and the mainland shoreline, there is a small jumble of round boulders seemingly abandoned in the sand like a giant's marbles. This tiny oasis is perhaps the highlight of the entire trip as it is absolutely stuffed full with tiny moray eels, Durban Shrimps (*Rhynchocinetes durbanensis*), colourful Tubastrea, Glassy Sweepers (*Pempheris schomburgkii*), angelfish and many anemones with Clark's Anemonefish (*Amphiprion clarkii*) in them. Much of the diving around

Above: *Various species of snapper enjoy shaded regions in coral overhangs, where they prey on small fish and crustaceans. Usually quite shy, some school in small groups, others prefer to hunt individually.*

Mahé is in fairly shallow water and while the reefs are not brilliant, they are more than made up for by a seemingly endless number of tropical fish. One of my favourite sites is **Whale Rocks**: huge granite blocks with a unique white gorgonian sea fan and fields of huge plate anemones each with their symbiotic partners, skunk clownfish.

There are three dives which are classed as long-range adventure dive sites. These are **Brissare Rocks**, **Shark Bank** and the *Ennerdale* wreck.

Brissare Rocks is an exposed, off-shore pinnacle virtually smothered in fire coral and home to countless species of fish. There is often a strong current, so additional care should be taken with your buoyancy and position. Shark Bank is a series of massive granite pillars which are a natural focus for fish with many schools of ocean travellers coming to feed and be cleaned. The walls are covered with orange sponges and white gorgonians. Orange Cup Corals (*Balanophyllia elegans*) continue the theme and in fact the whole area is strangely orange and white coloured, with even bare patches of granite sparkling lightly. Large pelagics are nearly always seen here and mackerel which always arrive before the Whale Sharks feeding on the plankton.

The *Ennerdale*

Originally built in 1963, the *Ennerdale* was a British Royal Navy Fleet Auxiliary Motor Tanker, chartered to the RAF in 1967. Loaded with 42,165 tonnes (41,500 tons) of refined furnace oil and gasoil, she struck an uncharted rock 11 km (7 miles) from port on 1 June 1970, badly holing her starboard side and she quickly sank. Releasing only small quantities of her cargo into the water, the oil was cleared by the Royal Navy before it could do damage to any of the inshore reefs around the islands. Deemed as a hazard to shipping, the ship was then bombed and dispersed.

As you descend to the ship down the shotline, the visibility is around 15 m (50 ft) and you know that you are getting close to the wreckage when the water column soon becomes crowded with large schools of Longfin Batfish (*Platax tiera*), various snapper and small jacks. Since the ship was a tanker, there are huge pipes everywhere, now covered in fire corals and small sponges. If you do manage to get to the crumpled bows, there are often sharks and stingrays hiding out in the overhangs.

Above: The Spanish Dancer (Hexabranchus sanguineus) is often found roaming the Seychelles reefs during daylight hours. The species here are more orange in colour. If you look closely, you may find a pair of symbiotic shrimps which live their lives on these large nudibranchs.

Amirantes

The Amirantes are a group of coral islands located 320 km (200 miles) southwest of the main Seychelles group; the largest is **Desroches** where much of the diving is concentrated.

Desroches is situated at the southern side of a huge atoll which was once the tip of an ancient volcano. Divers are taken across the shallow lagoon to the outer edge of the atoll wall. Virtually the entire wall is undercut with huge coral slabs creating caverns and interesting nooks and crannies for garish soldierfish and small schools of hatchetfish to hide out in. Brilliant red gorgonian sea fans stretch out into the current and whip-like black corals hold hidden secrets of blennies and tiny shrimps.

On the southeastern edge of the atoll the reef drops into a depression due to the collapse of some ancient underground/underwater cavern. Known locally as **The Boulders**, at only around 12 m (40 ft) deep, the outer edge drops away in a tumble of coral boulders eventually reaching the old coral rubble slope at over 30 m (100 ft). There are numerous caves and caverns which are host to Oriental Sweetlips (*Plectorhinchus orientalis*), squirrelfish and small groups of Glassy Sweepers with the usual attendant lionfish waiting on the sidelines to pick off strays. This ancient limestone reef has been sculpted by waves and weather over the centuries, creating a backdrop to scuba diving which is quite unlike any other area of the Seychelles.

Opposite: Huge circular caverns are carved into the reef top where you can descend and gain access to the mini-wall through long narrow tunnels. They are a spectacular start to the dive.

Above: Desroches, the largest island in the Amirantes Archipelago is located on the southern edge of a massive coral atoll. Cut with curious circular caves and caverns, this ancient mountaintop is home to species of fish, corals and invertebrates not found in the northern group.

Aldabra

Aldabra is the world's largest coral atoll and is a UNESCO World Heritage Site. Located 1,150 km (715 miles) southwest of Mahé, the only way to dive the region is by live-aboard private charter as dive boats rarely venture this far south due to security issues. Once a huge airforce base, the only flying done now is by the thousands of seabirds who thrive in this solitude. Much of the diving is concentrated around the main channel where millions of gallons of water rush in and out of the lagoon with the tides.

Mozambique

Mozambique was colonized by Portugal in 1505 after it wrested the country from the Arabs. Largely autonomous, Portuguese businessmen built their economy on slavery and exploitation of the country's resources. Inevitably the indigenous population rose up against these companies and waged a guerrilla war against Portuguese rule. A military junta took over the country in 1974 and Mozambique finally became independent in 1975. Portuguese is the main language spoken, as well as the local vernaculars which are a mix of Swahili, Makhuwa and Sena.

Mozambique's marine life has long enjoyed protection. Its ocean border is over 2,500 km (1,550 miles) long and lies between the Equatorial tropical zone and South African subtropical zone. Happily, it has escaped the coral bleaching caused by the dramatic rise in sea temperatures in 1998 which affected so much of the Seychelles and the Maldives.

Imagine the longest beach that you have ever seen, then multiply it several times over. The coastline of Mozambique has the largest sand dunes in the world and the longest beach you can dream of. These sand dunes continue underwater until they meet the outer reefs. Now that tourism has been accepted and the politicians have given up Marxism and espoused capitalism, Mozambique is advertising itself as one of the main shark diving destinations. Because it can also offer land-based safaris, the future of its tourism industry looks assured.

Opposite: Clockwise from top left: hawkfish hide amidst sponges and corals waiting for prey; local fishermen haul up their boat along Mozambique's never-ending beach; these boats are also used to carry divers; Regal Angelfish (Pygoplites diacanthus) are one of the more colourful angelfish found on Mozambique's reefs; seeing Whale Sharks (Rhincodon typus) is what divers come for.

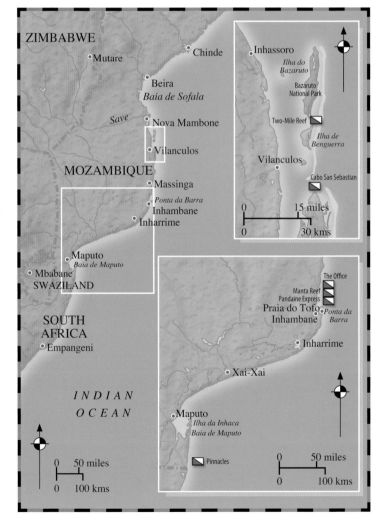

TRAVEL ADVISORY MOZAMBIQUE

Climate: Cool and dry in the winter months from April to September, with very little rain and daytime temperatures on the coast range around 24–27° C (75–80° F). The summer months from December to March are usually hot, sticky and rainy with electrical storms many afternoons, preceded by humid build-ups in the mornings. Rainfall of well over 200 mm (8 in) a month can be received. Temperatures generally range from 27–31° C (80–88° F).

When to go: Whale Shark season is usually from February to May and sometimes the annual sardine run will come as far north as this coastline, bringing the chance to see thousands of fish, sharks and whales.

Getting there: Flights to Maputo are regular and usually serviced from either South Africa or Kenya. You can fly up to Vilanculos opposite the Bazaruto Archipelago, but for those going to Ponta da Barra, it is a long drive up the EN1.

Water temperature: Averages 27° C (80° F) in summer, 20° C (68° F) in winter. Visibility is entirely variable due to the tidal currents; an incoming tide is always clearer.

Quality of marine life: Superb with plenty of chances for encounters with oceanic species including lots of shark species. The juvenile species of fish, five different varieties of seahorse and the mangrove communities are well worth the effort to discover.

Depth of dives: Averages around 6–25 m (20–80 ft) but a few of the offshore sites are much deeper.

Dive practicalities: Divers should wear full suits to avoid being stung by microscopic creatures, particularly in the shallow lagoons and mangroves.

Bazaruto Archipelago

The **Parque Nacional do Bazaruto** (Bazaruto National Park) is situated midway between Maputo in the south and Beira in the north. There are just a small handful of islands in the archipelago with the largest, Ilha do Bazaruto, in the north, Santa Carolina (Paradise Island) to the west and Ilha de Benguerra, Ilha de Magaruque and the tiny Ilha de Banqué in the south. The coral reefs run parallel to the shore and form a barrier on the east coast of the archipelago which is incredibly intricate in structure. Carved by tides and storms, there are literally thousands of small caves and caverns, swimthroughs, fissures, valleys and ridges, all covered with delicate corals and sponges.

Two Mile Reef is midway between Bazaruto and Benguerra and is exposed at low tide. Visibility is variable depending on the state of the tide. It is better to have a drift dive on the incoming tide as not only does it bring in much clearer water, it also brings in some of the larger predatory and game fish, such as jacks, barracuda and various sharks. The reef is undercut with many overhanging ledges draped with small soft corals, bubble and cup corals. While these reefs cannot be compared with the best of Indonesia or the Red Sea, they are truly magical and are some of the most pristine in the region.

Above: Eagle rays are a common hunter amidst the shallow sandbars that form at the mouth of the rivers and mangrove lagoons. They look for crustaceans and burrowing sea urchins.

North of Ponto San Sebastian is **Cabo San Sebastian**, a small rising reef structure around 30 m (100 ft) deep. This small ridge acts as a natural focus for all the game fish which pass through the Mozambique Channel. There are literally tons of fish to be found here with Manta Rays, Grey Reef Sharks, trevallies, huge Potato Cod (*Epinephelus tukula*) and tuna. The water column appears full as the various species of fish feed at different levels.

Ponta da Barra

Ponta da Barra is around 400 km (250 miles) north of the capital Maputo. The region has expansive mangrove forests, low sandbar islands, protected shallow bays and lagoons. There is a large tidal range here which suits the mangroves and this is a perfect opportunity to dive in the bay and view the complex structure and ecosystem which supports the mangroves and its inhabitants. The roots are a natural hatchery for many species of reef fish and juvenile snapper, butterflyfish and angelfish can be found everywhere. Tiny shells and worms, nudibranchs, starfish and sea urchins make their home on the root stems amid colourful algae and encrusting sponges. It is often better to do this lazy snorkel and dive on an incoming tide as the water is much clearer as it sweeps into the bay.

Opposite: Pyjama nudibranchs (Nembrotha purpureolineolata) *are just one of the many different, colourful species to be found on the shallow coral reefs. These feed mainly on sponges.*

About 15 km (9½ miles) northeast of Ponta da Barra is a dive site known as **The Office**. The maximum depth here is still only 25 m (80 ft) and there are low-lying coral heads topped with good growths of hard and soft corals and the underhangs are filled with schools of Bigeye Snapper (*Lutjanus lutjanus*), squirrelfish and large grouper. Delicate moray eels are all over, as are numerous cleaning stations manned by small wrasse, blennies and shrimps. Oceanic fish always visit this site and it is known for sightings of Manta Rays (*Manta birostris*), devil rays, Leopard Sharks (*Triakis semifasciata*), Grey Reef Sharks (*Carcharhinus amblyrhynchos*) and huge grouper. On nearby **Manta Reef**, two new subspecies of Manta Rays have been discovered since 2009 and are yet to be classified. Shark fiends usually prefer the top two shark reefs: **Pinnacles** and **Pandaine Express**. The corals aren't great here, but you are really coming to see the Bull (*Carcharhinus leucas*), Silvertip (*Carcharhinus albimarginatus*) and Blacktip Reef Sharks (*Carcharhinus melanopterus*). Both of these dives are fairly deep at over 30 m (100 ft) so bottom time is limited.

Above: Durban Hingeback Shrimps (Rhynchocinetes durbanensis) *are found in their multitudes during night dives. Always shy during the day, they appear to pose for the photographer at night.*

Opposite: Bearded Scorpionfish (Scorpaenopsis barbata), *the masters of disguise, lie in wait in the shallows for prey to pass close by.*

Western Australia

Almost a third of Australia's coastline is found in Western Australia and the range of biodiversity along this 7,000 km (4,700 mile) stretch is staggering. There are tropical coral reefs in the north, while well offshore are the Cocos Keeling Archipelago, Rowley Shoals, Scott Reef, Seringatapam Reef and Christmas Island. Although remote and difficult to get to without private charter, they offer some excellent diving opportunities. As you travel south towards Exmouth, the Ningaloo Reef is the longest fringing reef in the world.

Perth and the southwest have much cooler, temperate waters and there are several marine parks in the region which offer a hugely different biodiversity of invertebrates, sponges and algae. Wrecks litter the coast, both historical and deliberate as part of an artificial reef programme. Nearby Rottnest Island, 18 km (11 miles) to the west of Fremantle, has some superb dive sites. Two warships, HMAS *Swan* and HMAS *Perth* are now home to masses of marine life. About 60 km (37 miles) west of Geraldton off the mid-west coast are the Houtman Abrolhos Islands with some of the southernmost coral reefs in the Indian Ocean.

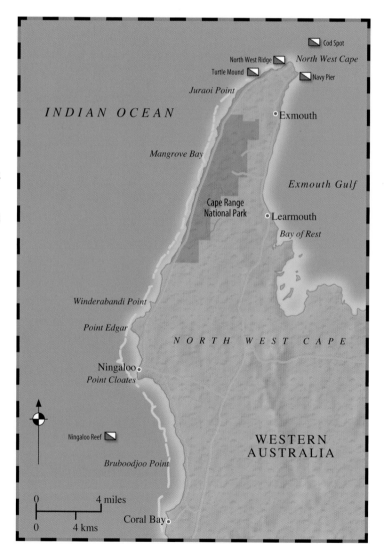

TRAVEL ADVISORY WESTERN AUSTRALIA

Climate: Tropical in the north with land temperatures varying from 26–30° C (79–86° F). Coral Bay further south will get up to 38° C (100° F).

When to go: Between April and November is best for the reef, April to June for Whale Sharks and August to October for the chance to see migrating whales.

Getting there: Flights to Perth and then up to Exmouth are frequent and easy. Most international carriers will get you to Perth.

Water temperature: Averages 22–29° C (71–84° F) throughout the year with visibility averaging around 15 m (50 ft)

Quality of marine life: Divers come for the Whale Sharks, which are always great (if they behave!). The reefs are interesting, but nothing like the tropical reefs further north.

Depth of dives: Averages around 15 m (50 ft) but most dives on the outer reefs will be much deeper. Whale Shark encounters are always by snorkelling only. In fact snorkelling some of the shallower inside sections and lagoons within Ningaloo is always great.

Dive practicalities: Much of the diving is drift diving, but there is usually a lot of hanging around waiting for the spotter planes to signal when the Whale Sharks are getting close. Full suits should be worn for protection, but when the water is warm, many just use swimwear.

Ningaloo Marine Park

Ningaloo Reef is where most divers want to go. It was declared a Marine Park in 1987. At over 260 km (162 miles) long, its principal attraction is the encounters with migrating Whale Sharks (*Rhincodon typus*). But there are always plenty of other opportunities for good scuba diving in Coral Bay and Turquoise Bay where depths rarely drop below 20 m (65 ft).

The Whale Sharks appear to time their arrival at Ningaloo with the coral spawning in March and usually stay in the area feeding until June, when the water temperatures start to rise. This massive spawning may literally turn the sea pink with eggs, visibility drops and the spotter planes are kept busy directing traffic to the feeding giants. The absolute thrill of swimming with the largest fish in the sea is an unforgettable and humbling experience as is the interaction with hundreds of remoras, Cobia (*Rachycentron canadum*), juvenile Golden Trevally (*Gnathanodon speciosus*) and thousands of jacks swarming around the sharks, all feeding on the rich soup of stinging plankton and ctenophores.

There is of course much more to Ningaloo than Whale Sharks with divers regularly enjoying over 500 species of fish; 600 species of molluscs; and three different species of turtle. Dugongs (*Dugong dugon*), Manta Rays (*Manta birostris*), eagle rays and schools of dolphins are also regularly encountered.

Off the Cape Range National Park around Exmouth's north-pointing headland are a number of popular local dive sites. **Cod Spot** has large and friendly Potato Cod (*Epinephelus tukula*); the **Navy Pier** is great for nudibranchs and small shrimp and gobies; **North West Ridge** will usually yield an encounter with big schools of trevally and jacks which come in close to feed on the schools of chromis and basslets; **Turtle Mound** has – you guessed it – great encounters with turtles when they are feeding on the turtle grass meadows in the shallows.

Previous page: Clockwise from top left: large coral bommies provide shelter for many species of fish; the coral species on these reefs are colourful and varied; tropical butterflyfish and angelfish are always a highlight of every dive; lionfish are one of the most adaptable predators of small reef fish in the Indian Ocean.

Above: Valentine's Pufferfish (Canthigaster valentini), often in pairs, are comical little reef dwellers, always foraging for small crustaceans amidst the coral polyps and algae formations.

Opposite: When you do find your Whale Shark (Rhincodon typus), it takes stamina and patience to keep up with them and to try and duck-dive to take photographs, while they are feeding.

Indo-Pacific

The name instantly identifies the location of this bridge between two of the most important zones on the planet. With the Pacific Ocean to the east and the Indian Ocean to the west, the islands found here are recognized worldwide as being at the hub of all marine life. Many aeons ago life arose here and developed on the young planet. As the tectonic plates shifted, so marine life spread around the world, though tidal currents and the building of shipping canals have also played their part. Surprisingly, identical species are found in the Caribbean and in the Indo-Pacific, testimony to the great age of these species and their primal origins.

Graced with beautiful coral reefs encircling the white sand shores of tropical islands, there are also massive movements of cold water travelling through the region in deep fissures bringing upwellings of nutrient-rich water on which the corals and all other marine life depend.

Above: Longnose Hawkfish (Oxycirrhites typus) *live almost exclusively on large gorgonian sea fans and black corals.*

Left: Colourful soft corals and beautiful tropical fish in abundance are the main pleasures for many divers.

Thailand

Lying within the tropical northern hemisphere, the kingdom of Thailand spans roughly 16 degrees of latitude. It has perhaps the most diverse climate in South-East Asia and its topography ranges from high forested mountains in the north to tropical coral islets in the south, as well as the curious and dramatic karst limestone islets. Many of the offshore islands are granitic in origin. These rocky islands have more low encrusting corals and leathery corals than the tropical reefs of central Malaysia and Indonesia.

Thailand is bathed by the waters of both the eastern Indian Ocean and the Andaman Sea to the west and the Gulf of Thailand to the east. Most of the diving takes place in the Andaman Sea. There are huge numbers of diving centres, but many opt for live-aboard dive boats which can explore further out into the Andaman Sea and visit some truly superb diving locations.

The corals are abundant and pristine, the fish life varied and interesting and as much attention can be profitably given to the little critters as to the pelagic encounters with larger species.

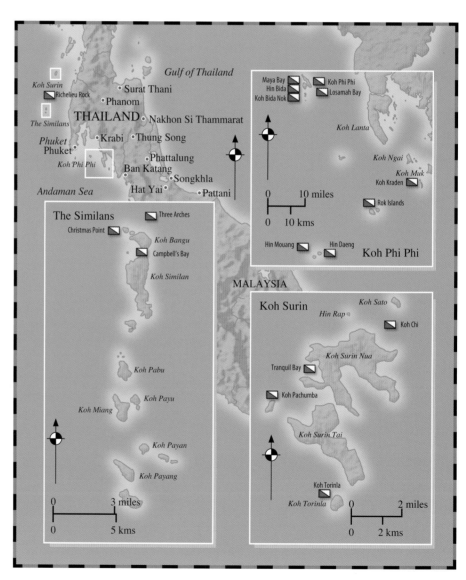

TRAVEL ADVISORY THAILAND

Climate: 28–34° C (82–93° F) with the northwest monsoon bringing ferocious storms during May to November. The best diving is around the offshore island marine parks, which experience much lower humidity than the mainland and usually have light sea breezes.

When to go: Most dive boats either move to the Gulf of Thailand or are laid up in the monsoon season with the best months being November through March.

Getting there: Flights to Bangkok and Phuket are available from most international destinations.

Water temperature: Averages 28° C (82° F) in summer, 26° C (79° F) in winter. Visibility is usually around 12–18 m (40–60 ft).

Quality of marine life: Superb, with a very high chance of encountering large pelagics. Be aware that this is not a region for lush coral growth as the underwater terrain is all made of granite boulders, many of which appear impervious to colonization by more delicate corals.

Depth of dives: Averages around 18 m (60 ft) and rarely over 30 m (100 ft) making it perfect for all levels of diver and for those wishing to learn to dive.

Dive practicalities: Some of the offshore islands are prone to strong currents. Full suits are advised as there are plenty of microscopic stinging things in the plankton, as well as small stinging hydroids attached to the granite boulders.

Mu Koh Surin Marine National Park

Mu Koh Surin Marine National Park consists of five large granite islands and numerous small rocky islets covering some 135 sq km (52 sq miles) of water. The largest of the islands is **Koh Surin Nua**, then comes **Koh Surin Tai** which can be reached at low tide when the 200 m (660 ft) gap is shallow enough to walk across. Uninhabited except for the park rangers and itinerant sea gypsies, the islands are only visited by the live-aboard dive boats which operate from Koh Phuket. All of the dive sites have suffered from dynamite fishing in the past and much of this damage is still very obvious, but thankfully the region is now fully protected.

To the northwest is **Koh Chi** or **Nun Rock** which is quite a deep dive as the boulders are all low lying at depths of around 18–25 m (60–80 ft) It is best known for it sightings of large pelagics including Bigeye Trevallies (*Caranx sexfasciatus*), tuna and big schools of barracuda. To the west of Koh Surin Nua is **Tranquil Bay** which is only used as a night diving location as the bottom is, at most, just 15 m (50 ft) below the dive boat. There are always plenty of nocturnal animals and fish to be found here and the lower rocks are brilliantly coloured by Golden Cup Corals (*Tubastraea aurea*) and small fan worms.

Below: Shy Green Chromis (Chromis viridis) duck into Acropora coral for protection when you get too close to them. Mainly feeding on plankton, they hide deep in the coral recesses at night.

The dive at **Koh Pachumba** (Dragon Island) is around a small submerged pinnacle which rises from 21 m (70 ft) to just 4 m (13 ft) below the surface. It is not a great site for marine life and the boulders are covered more with sponges than corals, but several species of shark are found in the vicinity. **Koh Torinla** off the southwest tip of Koh Surin Tai is a superb, diverse site as it features granite boulders, good coral formations, small buttress reefs and mini-walls. Large anemones are found in shallower waters with at least three or four different anemone fish. The corals are alive with brilliantly coloured chromis and damselfish. The maximum depth here is only 27 m (90 ft) but most divers prefer to stay in the shallower sections as there is just so much going on.

Richelieu Rock

Widely renowned as one of the world's elite dives, **Richelieu Rock** in the marine sanctuary is regarded as Thailand's number one dive site. More regularly visited by live-aboard dive boat, when weather and sea conditions are perfect it can be reached via a three-hour boat trip from Khurauri Pier. Visible only at low tide, the granite and coral pinnacles are prone to currents and the visibility is extremely variable. The main pinnacle has vertical walls and is surrounded by numerous smaller pinnacles which reach almost to the surface. The depth drops to 45 m (150 ft) but most divers just meander around the outcrops of coral-encrusted granite at the 18 m (60 ft) depth range to get maximum bottom time.

Because Richelieu Rock is so isolated, it invariably attracts large schools of fish to feed and be cleaned in the shallows and inevitably this also attracts the larger pelagics such as sunfish, Whale Sharks (*Rhincodon typus*) and Manta Rays (*Manta birostris*). While most divers come to look for the big critters, the shallower boulders and corals are absolutely teeming with life and you can find most species recorded in Thai waters given enough time. Most live-aboard dive boats will spend the day here to allow you to get your fill of a superb offshore location.

Above: The offshore granite islands are smothered in encrusting leather corals and sponges.

Mu Koh Similan Marine National Park

This small archipelago of nine larger granitic islands and many small seamounts and rocks is uninhabited except for the park rangers. Due to the Similans' geographical location, the eastern shores are more sheltered from any monsoons and have quiet coves (perfect for dive boats) and sandy lagoons, whereas the exposed western shores are rugged and battered, bearing the full force of the monsoons between May and November. The western dive sites comprise large jumbles of boulders which drop down 40 m (135 ft) or more compared to the much shallower and sheltered east coast which has superb coral gardens.

In late spring, around March and April, the sea temperature rises as the plankton bloom, which reduces the visibility. However, this is also when most sightings of Whale Sharks and Manta Rays occur as they are here to 'hoover' up this free harvest.

Koh Bangu in the north has a superb dramatic site called the **Three Arches** or the **Golden Arches** named after the rocky arches which have been formed when boulders have toppled over. Visibility is not that great here as the surrounding waters are quite shallow at only around 27 m (90 ft). Large sea cucumbers and sea urchins are found grazing on the low algae and the crevices have the usual schools of sweetlips, hatchetfish, Glassy Sweepers (*Pempheris schomburgkii*) and squirrelfish. Off Koh Bangu's western point is **Christmas Point**, again featuring large boulders. These have created numerous swimthroughs where soft corals cling and small sea fans filter the current. Look out for the juvenile Rockmover Wrasse (*Novaculichthys taeniourus*) and sweetlips as they undulate around the overhangs.

Continuing south around Koh Similan, **Campbell's Bay** in the north is favoured by the live-aboard boats as it is fairly sheltered and able to offer easy night diving from the moorings. The usual boulders and small coral heads are found scattered over a wide sandy seabed at only around 12 m (40 ft) in depth making it a perfect place to spend time exploring all the little crevices for small shells, nudibranchs, octopus and squid.

Above: Royal nudibranchs (Chromodoris bullocki) are well named. Particularly colourful with a purple body, golden tentacles and gills and a white-spotted skirt, they are always a delight to find.

Left: Nudibranchs are some of the most exotic and colourful of all the marine invertebrates found underwater. They have a variety of diets including sponges, anemones, coral polyps, stinging hydroids and algae. They are able to store their prey's stinging cells inside their own body for added protection. Generally the more colourful they are, the more toxic they are

Below: Gorgonian sea fans align themselves perpendicularly to the current to filter-feed on the plankton as it passes around these offshore islands.

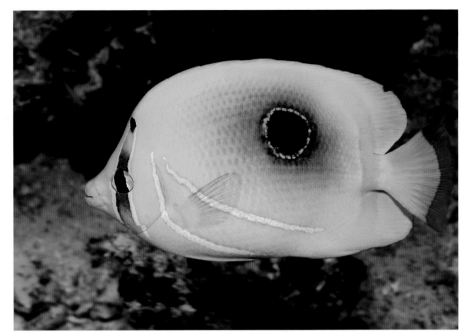

Left: *There are more than 120 species of butterflyfish worldwide, most of which are found in the Indo-Pacific zone. All of them are incredibly colourful and most have very striking markings, such as this Eclipse Butterflyfish (Chaetodon bennetti).*

Koh Lanta Marine National Park

Opposite above: *Invariably, the further offshore the dive site, the better chance there is to see large pelagics such as Whale Sharks (Rhincodon typus) and Manta Rays (Manta birostris).*

Located in the Koh Lanta Marine National Park, **Hin Mouang** (Purple Rock) and **Hin Daeng** (Red Rock) are the only two open ocean reef structures in this area. They are over five hours by dive boat from Saladin Pier, so the site is more favoured by the live-aboard dive boats working out from Koh Phuket. Currents are usually quite strong and prone to changing direction around these offshore granitic seamounts. Hin Mouang consists of around six or more pinnacles with the shallowest coming to 8 m (26 ft) below the surface. The drop off here is one of the deepest in Thai waters reaching over 70 m (235 ft) and therefore beyond most sport diving limits. Reef sharks are commonplace among the pinnacles which are home to a superb display of soft and hard corals. Only 500 m (1,650 ft) away is Hin Daeng. It is shallower than Hin Mouang with a maximum depth of around 35 m (115 ft) and the rocky formations are more like huge slabs creating mini-walls and small shelves, thus allowing better soft and hard coral growth. Again, it is the good chance of pelagic encounters which attracts divers.

Other great dive sites nearby are **Rok Islands** to the northeast, shallower in depth at only 20 m (66 ft) maximum and often used by the dive boats for night diving. At Koh Rok Nok there is an underground freshwater stream which comes out amid the jumble of boulders. The only shipwreck in the area is thought to be that of a Japanese destroyer sunk in the Second World War. Known as the *Koh Kraden* wreck, it is well broken up, and the visibility is generally quite poor in this region due to river water run-off. The wreck is really only for experienced divers as it is prone to silting and covered in old fishing nets.

Opposite below: *Large barrel sponges dot the reef slopes amidst colourful gorgonians and leather corals. Look closely at the sponges for small eels, crabs and shrimps. These large formations make excellent homes for many marine creatures.*

Koh Phi Phi Marine National Park

Koh Bida Nok and **Hin Bida** have long been well known to divers as they are so close to Phuket Town but most divers stay on the largest of the islands, Koh Phi Phi Don. All of the diving is done from the pier here and the local dive sites are only a short 15-minute boat ride away. Two sites, Hin Phae and Hin Dot, are usually used as shallower dive sites on the return journey from Koh Bida Nok and Hin Bida to the southeast as the journey time can take as much as two hours depending on the boat used. Phi Phi Ley is the second largest island and is uninhabited as the cliffs are so precipitous. Dives are done here in **Maya Bay** and **Losamah Bay** as they are such sheltered locations, but they do have strong currents which allow for some exciting drift dives.

Koh Bida Nok is the largest of the two granite outcrops directly south of Phi Phi Ley and features huge granite boulders tumbling to around 20 m (66 ft). There are many large gorgonians found here and the soft corals appear to be even richer and more colourful than in other locations. The flatter ledges have large anemones and the usual host of clownfish and damselfish, and there are tons of basslets just stretching out to feed on the plankton. Sharks and rays are found nearer the seabed and most crevices and overhangs have lionfish and scorpionfish.

A further 8 km (5 miles) southeast is Hin Bida or Shark Point as it is referred to locally. The rock is only 1 m (3 ft) above the surface. This is actually a nice easy dive as the depth is only 20 m (66 ft) with not much current. The sharks of Shark Point are actually Leopard Sharks (*Stegostoma fasciatum*) and lots are usually seen in the vicinity. During mating, the male grabs the extended tail of the female and soon they are writhing all over the seabed breaking small corals and sponges!

Opposite above: Small reef blennies and gobies always strike comical poses for the photographer on the tips of coral heads.

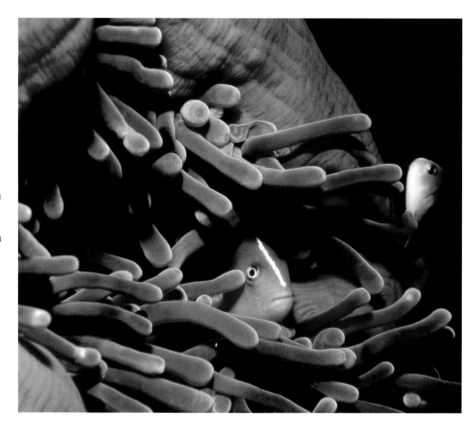

Above: Clownfish or anemonefish retreat inside their host anemones whenever danger threatens. They are immune to the anemones' stinging cells.

Opposite: Ocellate Phyllidia (Phyllidia ocellata) are related to the true nudibranchs but do not have the external gills more commonly seen.

Malaysia

Malaysia is a vast country divided into two parts that are separated by the South China Sea. One part is the Malay peninsula to the south of and bordering Thailand; the other, comprising the states of Sabah and Sarawak, is located on the north of Borneo, one of the largest islands in the Indo-Pacific region. To the west of the peninsula there are a number of offshore island resorts, such as Penang and Langkawi. The east coast yields superb white sand beaches that shelve into the clear waters where coral 'jungles' are found. Not only is the country ethnically and culturally diverse, the marine life found in these waters is also incredibly varied.

All of Malaysia's islands lie on the continental shelf and have depths averaging only 100 m (330 ft). Between the edge of the continental shelf and Sipadan lies a trough 1,000 m (3,280 ft) deep. The living reef that we are privileged to see is only the top 50 m (165ft) or so, but its profile and other characteristics are influenced by the deep and precipitous nature of the island.

Most of the smaller islands have superb hotel resorts or villages which are built out into the sea. All of them have excellent, professionally run diving resorts and while most of them have dive sites and house reefs close at hand, many will also venture further afield to neighbouring islands where the reefs and coral walls are spectacular.

Opposite: Clockwise from top left; resting or sleeping turtles are a common site on the coral ledges of the wall; the vertical walls, covered in marine life, stretch down into infinity; Bumphead Parrotfish (Bolbometopan muricatum) are seen in large groups in the evenings, biting off 'fist-sized' chunks of coral to eat the polyps within; schools of trevally tolerate divers by moving around them in large circular formations.

Below: Pulau Sipadan once hosted several dive resorts but the island is now a turtle and bird reserve under the protection of the Malaysian Government. The reef wall drops precipitously directly from the shore and this huge mushroom-shaped coral mountain top is riddled with deep caves and caverns.

TRAVEL ADVISORY PENINSULAR MALAYSIA

Climate: 23–34° C (73–93° F) with the northeast monsoon bringing wetter weather from November to March. Typhoons are possible from August to November, but in general you do take your chances on any of these offshore islands and rain should be expected anytime.

When to go: Generally from April to October as many resorts may close during monsoon season.

Getting there: Access to the islands is mainly by boat from either Marang or Kuala Terengganu and all of the resorts have their own transport. There is a small airport at Kuala Terengganu with flights from either Changi Airport in Singapore or Kuala Lumpur with Berjaya Air but with restricted baggage allowance.

Water temperature: Averages 28° C (82° F) in summer, 24° C (75° F) in winter. Visibility is usually around 30 m (100 ft).

Quality of marine life: Very good densities of reef fish around healthy shallow coral reefs.

Depth of dives: Averages around 18 m (60 ft) but with many shallow lagoons and beach locations is perfect for snorkelling.

Dive practicalities: There is a wide diversity of shallow reef and deeper wall dives, so buoyancy is always important.

TRAVEL ADVISORY SARAWAK/SABAH

Climate: 23–34° C (73–93° F) with the northeast monsoon bringing wetter weather from November to March. Typhoons are possible from August to November but in general you do take your chances on any of these offshore islands and rain should be expected anytime.

When to go: The best time to visit Layang-Layang, Pulau Sipadan, Mabul and Kapalai is between March and October. Note that most resorts are closed during the northeast monsoon, which blows from November to March. Layang-Layang is closed from September to February.

Getting there: Malaysian Airlines fly daily from Heathrow to Kuala Lumpur and Singapore. From there, Malaysian Airlines also operate an internal flight regularly to all other airports including Kota Kinabalu on Borneo where the rest of your transfers will be arranged for Mabul and Sipadan. There is a weight restriction of 20 kg (44 lb) per passenger on smaller domestic flights to the offshore island resorts, so pack frugally!

Water temperature: Averages 28° C (82° F) in summer, 24° C (75° F) in winter. Visibility is usually around 25–30 m (80–100 ft).

Quality of marine life: Greatest density and diversity of species in the region, being so close to the 'hub' of the Indo-Pacific.

Depth of dives: From the surface to depths well beyond the accepted limits of sport or recreational technical diving.

Dive practicalities: Wherever you are diving, you always need great buoyancy control to avoid damaging the coral and some form of protective clothing against fire coral and stinging hydroids. In the winter months, a thicker wetsuit is recommended. All dive resorts are able to offer diving instruction to all levels.

Pulau Redang

Pulau Redang is the largest of nine islands within the Terengganu Marine Park which is known worldwide and recognized as having one of the best coral reefs and marine ecosystems in peninsular Malaysia.

Dive sites are located mainly to the north, east and south with all of Pulau Redang's offshore islands and seamounts offering the best sites, except for **Turtle Bay** and **Teluk Dalam**. Turtle Bay to the north is a great place for turtles; however, the site is quite exposed and sea is often rough. Teluk Dalam is also good for turtles but there is better coral growth here, which is mostly low lying and encrusting. Fish life isn't abundant but there is a huge variety.

There can be strong currents off the point at **Tanjung Gua Kawah**, so this is for more experienced divers. However, the rewards of seeing large pelagics are excellent.

Big Mount is one of the favourite dives and is located 50 m (165 ft) off the northern tip of Pulau Lima to the east. This oval seamount has an average depth of 20 m (66 ft) and drops down a coral-encrusted boulder slope to 30 m (100 ft). Travelling south, **Mini Seamount** to the east of Pulaus Kerrengga Kecil and Besar has a maximum depth of only 20 m (66 ft) and there are great encrusting corals and sponges. Large barrel sponges are home to sea cucumbers and plenty of parrotfish and wrasse.

Northeast Corner at Pulau Ekor Tebu is another large boulder slope dive site which bottoms out at around 24 m (80 ft). There is a large cavern that is always worth exploring and Blacktip Reef Sharks (*Carcharhinus melanopterus*) are usually found here.

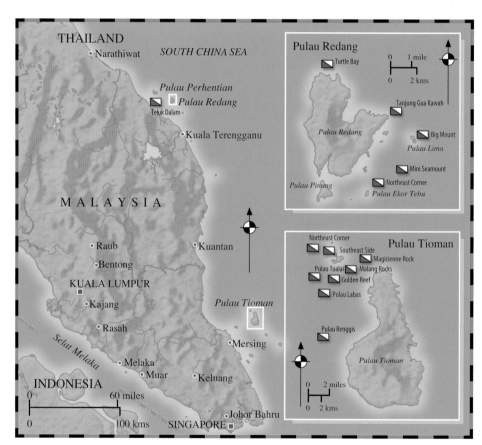

Pulau Tioman

Pulau Tioman is the largest of a group of 64 volcanic islands in the Seri Buat archipelago. The diving is found mainly off the northwest coast.

Amazingly this more southerly location is more prolific than the northern peninsula with common sightings of Manta Rays (*Manta birostris*) and Whale Sharks (*Rhincodon typus*) around April to June when the northern plankton bloom is at its strongest. There are also some superb huge jellyfish at this time. This also means that the visibility may be reduced but the offshore islands of Pulau Chebeh, Pulau Tulai and Pulau Sepoi usually have good visibility all season.

Pulau Chebeh's Northeast Corner has some huge volcanic boulders which drop down to 27 m (90 ft) There are plenty of low lying encrusting corals, as expected, yet there are also good stands of gorgonians, soft corals and plenty of reef fish and invertebrates. On the **Southeast Side** dive site there are usually strong currents on the surface and you drop down to the boulder-strewn dive site via a shotline. The average depth is 18 m (60 ft) and divers will enjoy some superb sea fans. **Pulau Tualai**, **Pulau Labas** and **Magicienne Rock** are also similar with large boulders encrusted with leather corals and small sea fans dropping to a sandy seabed. There are always plenty of butterfly and angelfish found on these sites. **Malang Rocks** and **Golden Reef** are shallower sites with Malang Rocks favoured by snorkellers. Near the Berjaya Resort is **Pulau Renggis** which is often favoured for night diving as it is the closest good reef to the dive centres.

Above: Leather corals, soft corals and acropora hard corals are common in this area as well as large schools of reef fish.

Layang-Layang Atoll

Off Borneo, to the northwest lies **Layang-Layang**, part of the Spratly archipelago, and on the eastern border with Indonesia the sister islands of Mabul, Kapalai and Sipadan are found. Located very close to the central hub of the Indo-Pacific where the diversity of marine life is at its richest, these tiny islands comprising some 8 ha (20 acres) of tropical rainforest are home to unique environments unrivalled anywhere else in Malaysia.

Northwest of Borneo are the Spratlys, comprising some 750 islands, seamounts and submerged shoals. Ownership is hotly contested by all the bordering countries and Malaysia claims the Layang-Layang Atoll where it has now established a naval base. Indirectly this base has served to protect the pristine coral reefs in this region from the more destructive fishing methods found nearby. Now served with its own airstrip, it is only a one-hour flight from Kota Kinabalu.

Layang-Layang Atoll consists of 13 linked coral reefs but is surrounded by the deep waters of the South China Sea with depths over 2,000 m (6,560 ft). This is one of the few oceanic locations where divers are virtually assured of sightings of large groups of Scalloped Hammerhead Sharks (*Sphyrna lewini*). All of the diving around Layang-Layang is wall diving, although there are drift dive forays into the lagoon, similar to those in Rangiroa in French Polynesia. All of the dives and access to them by boat are totally dependent on wind and weather as this will determine which part of the atoll is on the 'lee' side. There are some 20 dive sites around the atoll with **D'Wall** often coming out at the top of the list mainly during March when the large schools of hammerhead sharks are found.

Gorgonian Forest is obviously named after the huge gorgonian sea fans which stretch out into the prevailing currents. Usually surrounded by schools of anthias and small wrasse, they are over 2 m (6½ ft) in diameter. **Shark's Cave** usually has small Whitetip Reef Sharks (*Triaenodon obesus*) resting as well as patrolling Blacktip Reef Sharks (*Carcharhinus melanopterus*). Brilliantly coloured red squirrelfish are always found here as well as the usual shade-loving snapper and grunt. Although regarded as a rather unattractive site, **The Valley** is known for its huge coral boulders and superb soft corals which come in every colour imaginable.

Above: Fantastic colourful sea fans are synonymous with all of the walls in this region, as there is usually light to moderate current around most exposed sites, making it the perfect habitat for filtering plankton-rich waters.

Pulau Sipadan

Apart from the caves and caverns, **Pulau Sipadan** is justifiably famous for its precipitous reef wall. At the northern end of the island the drop-off starts just a few metres from the shore and is quite clearly indicated by the change in water colour from a pale green in the shallows to that intense cobalt blue which you only find when a reef wall plunges hundreds of metres to the seabed far below. Many divers have their first view of the majesty of Sipadan directly under the old pier.

Continuing around the island in a clockwise pattern, **Barracuda Point** is usually at the top of most people's dive list. A coral buttress stretches out northwards to the abyss and there is a shallow coral valley where Leopard Sharks (*Stegostoma fasciatum*) are usually encountered. Most people opt for the outer wall where you do see large schools of barracuda and jacks.

There are many sites around this small island and all of them are worth diving, such as the **Coral Gardens** where acres of large gorgonian sea fans stretch out into the current. **White Tip Avenue**, **Mid Reef**, **Turtle Patch** and **South Point** are all well known for their Whitetip Reef Sharks. **Staghorn Crest** is, as the name implies, a field of good quality Staghorn Coral (*Acropora formosa*) which are filled with anthias and damselfish. **Lobster Lairs** and **Hanging Gardens** on the western side of the island are more undercut with many small caves and caverns and beautiful soft corals. **West Ridge** is a more vertical wall where jacks and Humphead Parrotfish (*Bolbometapon muricatum*) are common, but what we love to see most are the turtles.

In the 25 minutes it takes you to walk around the island, you are constantly aware of the craters and tracks in the sand created by the Green Sea Turtles (*Chelonia mydas*) and Hawksbill Turtles (*Eretmochelys imbricata*) which come up onto the beaches at Sipadan each night to lay their eggs.

Above: Large schools of barracuda are usually found off most exposed points, whilst found singly on reef edges. They congregate in large numbers, creating a swirling mass of silvery fish.

Pulau Mabul

On nearby **Mabul**, the diving sites aren't nearly as intense and don't even have such clear waters; however, on the house reefs in front of the dive resorts, the seabed has black or dark brown sand and the muck diving here is excellent.

It has gained an enviable reputation for having a huge diversity of little critters. To give just a small example of what is found on the house reef, there are frogfish, Harlequin Shrimps (*Hymenocera picta*), cuttlefish, Twinspot Gobies (*Signigobius biocellatus*), snake eels, nudibranchs by the score and curiously shaped scorpionfish. **Crocodile Avenue** doesn't have crocodiles but it does have Crocodilefish or Flatheads (*Cymbacephalus beauforti*) as well as Leaf Scorpionfish (*Taenianotus triacanthus*).

Nudibranch Centre to the south of the island is a five-minute boat ride and, you guessed it, there are tons of nudibranchs found here. Visibility is often poor and the reef always looks a bit drab, but this suits the nudibranchs. **Coral Reef Garden** has very good quality corals for those who do not want to take the trip to Sipadan, but the site is best dived in the morning for the sunlight which just seems to sparkle off the corals.

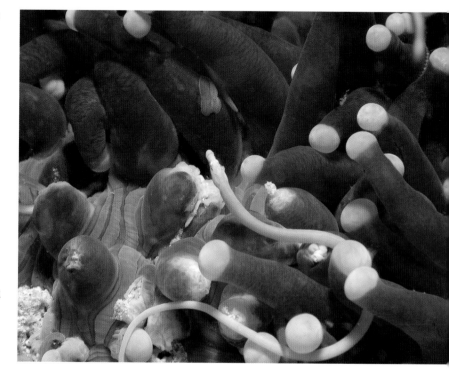

Above: *Curious Mushroom Pipefish (Siokunichthys nigrolineatus) and frogfish live among the scattered jetsam left over by the dive resort's construction workers.*

Pulau Kapalai

Actually, **Kapalai** isn't an island; rather it is a giant sandbank only seen at very low tides. The original sandy island has long since been eroded by tide and time. There are no large reef structures here but the site is perfect for spending plenty of bottom time and finding all of those weird and wonderful critters that we love. There are some 30 dive sites around the sandbank and while they cannot compare to the wall diving and crystal waters of nearby Sipadan, it is great for novice divers and photographers. **Cleaning Station** along the northeast ledge is worthy of note for the large number of cleaning wrasse which have set up shop on the reef to clean visiting fish of parasites. You will usually find queueing sweetlips and grouper here and quite often both predators and prey appear to suspend the lifelong pursuit of nature's game for a quick clean up!

Indonesia

Once considered a problematic destination due to political instability and lack of airline connections, Indonesia has rapidly become one of the top diving destinations in the world. A massive and diverse country with a simply staggering geographical range, the fantastic quality and quantity of marine life is unrivalled anywhere else in the world. Indonesia comprises some 17,500 islands ranging in size from tiny uninhabited islets to islands larger than most European countries.

Many of the northern islands are still heavily forested and much of the country is still relatively unexplored. In the south, much of the land has been cleared over the centuries for cultivation and it is these islands which also are most heavily populated.

Diving conditions are excellent overall, but divers should be aware of local tidal variations and currents, particularly in the south where the massive water movements between the islands produce incredibly strong currents. Not only is the region in the equatorial convergence zone of the main weather patterns from both northern and southern hemispheres, there are also deep water currents and upwellings from the Indian Ocean and the Pacific which rise in the northern regions of the South China Sea and travel southwards through the islands. They will affect almost every dive that you will do. However, for the most part, the diving is easy and colourful, the waters warm and inviting, and dive resorts professional with well-maintained boats and equipment. Many 'foreign' companies own dive resorts amid the islands, so standards are always very high.

Opposite: Clockwise from top left: many islands are known for their breeding turtles and young can often be found making a dash for the sea; caverns filled with brilliant red squirrelfish are common in all areas; Ornate Ghost Pipefish (Solenostomus paradoxus) are on many underwater photographers' wish list; the sheer variety of colourful soft corals and crinoids is simply staggering.

Above: The jetty on Gangga Island looks towards mainland Sulawesi over 40 minutes away by fast boat. These northern Indonesian reefs are regarded as world class.

TRAVEL ADVISORY KALIMANTAN

Climate: 28–34° C (82–93° F) with the remains of the northeast monsoon bringing wetter weather from December to March. The offshore islands are much less humid than the mainland and usually have light sea breezes.

When to go: Sangalaki is open all year round but March to August are considered peak months.

Getting there: Flights to Balikpapan are available from Kota Kinabalu, Singapore and Kuala Lumpur. From Balikpapan you then take a one-hour flight to Berau (Tanjung Redeb) and then a further two hours by boat to Sangalaki! Okay, not for the faint-hearted, but the trip is well worth the effort to stay in a small resort with only a maximum of 20 guests.

Water temperature: Averages 28° C (82° F) in summer, 26° C (79° F) in winter. Visibility is normally around 30 m (100 ft).

Quality of marine life: There are some 500 recorded species of soft and hard corals found here, with fish and invertebrates also prolific.

Depth of dives: Averages around 18 m (60 ft) but you will usually go much deeper.

Dive practicalities: There is a wide diversity of shallow reefs and with a maximum depth of only 18 m (60 ft) this is ideal for all levels of diver. There is a 2.5-m (8-ft) tidal range here which means that at high tide you can embark your boat on the shore, but at low tide you may have to walk more than 150 m (500 ft) to get to deeper water.

TRAVEL ADVISORY NORTHERN SULAWESI/IRIAN JAYA

Climate: 24–32° C (75–32° F) with the northeast monsoon bringing rain and strong winds from November to February.

When to go: Most of the resorts are open all year round but March to August are considered peak months. A large number of live-aboard dive boats operate in this region and these will explore further afield and in most cases you will be on virtually undived reefs.

Getting there: Flights to Manado are available from Kota Kinabalu, Singapore, Bali and Kuala Lumpur. Most of the dive resorts are within an hour's drive from the airport and pick-ups are always arranged by the resorts. For Irian Jaya, connecting flights are made through Sorong.

Water temperature: Averages 28° C (82° F) in summer, 26° C (79° F) in winter. Visibility is usually around 30 m (100 ft) except around the hot water vents off the north coast of Sulawesi.

Quality of marine life: Superb, with more weird fish and critters to be found here than anywhere else I know of.

Depth of dives: Averages around 18 m (60 ft) but you will usually go much deeper.

Dive practicalities: Currents are to be expected so always listen to the advice from your dive guides to make your diving safer and more interesting.

Sangalaki

Just two degrees north of the equator, **Sangalaki** is located in the Indonesian province of Kalimantan in Borneo. While it is only 190 km (120 miles) south of nearby Sipadan, Mabul and Kapalai, it is regarded as having much better diving than its northern counterparts. Virtually all the diving is either in or around the shallow lagoons or drift diving from the day dive boats at the entrances to the lagoon channels.

Sangalaki is a protected marine park, so all the reefs are in good condition. They start just a short distance from the island. **Sandy Ridge** is well known for its garden eels as well as interesting corals, but inevitably it is the Manta Rays (*Manta birostris*) that get your attention, depending on the direction of the currents. When they are moving southeast it is possible to visit two other dive sites – **Turtle Town** and either **Coral Gardens** or **Turtle Patch**. As the name implies, you will see turtles on these dives and while we are always ultra-aware of our buoyancy in the water so as not to damage the corals, turtles have no such qualms and are usually seen crashing through delicate corals to get at tasty sponges.

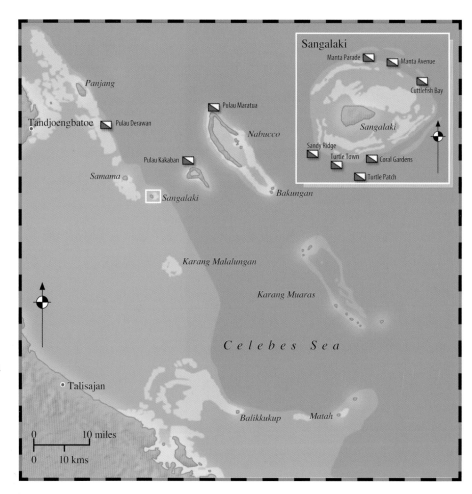

Around the northeastern reefs are **Manta Parade**, **Manta Avenue** and **Cuttlefish Bay**. You will usually see the beasts in question but these are generally in deeper water as the seabed slopes down to over 28 m (92 ft). Cuttlefish Bay is a gently sloping coral reef with many sandy patches and algae beds where cuttlefish come in to lay their eggs and feed on the small fish and shrimps which inhabit the area.

Travelling out from Sangalaki, some of the best diving at **Pulau Derawan** is along the end of the resort's pier which stretches out over 200 m (650 ft) on its southeast coast. Unfortunately the visibility is generally poor here, but do not let this put you off. Further to the west are **Pulau Kakaban** and **Pulau Maratua**. Visibility is always better here. Eagle rays are common, as are large numbers of sharks and Manta Rays as they make their way into and out of the lagoon. On Pulau Kakaban there is a Jellyfish Lake which rivals that found in Palau. Almost the entire size of the island, it can be reached by a 20-minute walk through the rainforest, so mosquito repellent is a must. There are four different species of non-stinging jellyfish as well as varieties of algae and small sponges and corals amid mangrove roots.

The island is also known for its macro photography subjects such as mantis shrimps, pipefish, Ornate Ghost Pipefish (*Solenostomus paradoxus*), seahorses and nudibranchs.

Below: Black crinoids hang precariously off gorgonian sea fans, as they spread their arms in the ever-present current between many islands.

Northern Sulawesi

Northern Sulawesi is the rather ragged-looking arm of the massive volcanic island that is roughly 'H' shaped. The region is acclaimed as having some of the most diverse marine life on the planet.

Gangga Island is a low-lying island with only one local village and a dive resort. Its lush green shores and crystal-clear waters are now legendary. Diving is from one of the traditional wooden boats, which range over a wide area.

There are only a couple of dive sites actually on Gangga Island as the water is so shallow and can have quite strong currents. However, you can find cuttlefish, tons of nudibranchs and the incredibly rare Pontohi Pygmy Seahorse

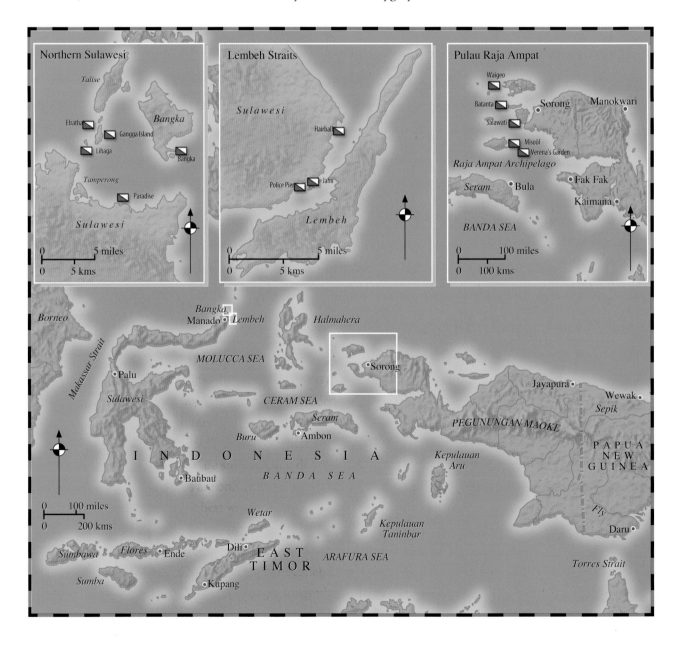

(*Hippocampus pontohi*). The closest large island to the east is **Bangka** and there are a number of exotic sites here with a couple of exhilarating drift dives along a superb coral reef. There are also two sites where you can dive through caves, caverns and pinnacles in offshore locations, all of which are superb. Jahir Dua is one such pinnacle which rises to just 6 m (20 ft) below the surface.

Directly south close to the northern coast of Sulawesi, there is a simply staggering dive called **Paradise** and nicknamed Little Lembeh! This is a black/brown sand muck dive but it is located out from an old wooden pier in front of a rather run-down resort. There are hot water vents which open up near the old resort's wooden pier. Curiously this seems to have encouraged the marine growth on the pilings and each wooden post is covered in exotic sponges, gorgonian sea fans and other soft and hard corals, all of which are home to Ornate Ghost Pipefish, frogfish, cleaner shrimps, various tunicates and hermit crabs. The volcanic hot water cools and spreads out over the reef as it drops down the mucky slope. The corals are in superb condition and you can find many exotic species of fish here as well as squid, cuttlefish, Mimic Octopus (*Thaumoctopus mimicus*) and other weird and wonderful muck dwellers.

The dives to catch the mating dance of the Mandarinfish (*Synchiropus splendidus*) are also excellent. Just two minutes by boat to the small deserted island of **Lihaga**, you will encounter a drab broken coral landscape made spectacular by the nightly courtship of the Mandarinfish.

The easy slope and mini-wall of **Efratha** are also exceptional. The wall is literally crammed with marine life where neon file clams and colourful nudibranchs vie for space with giant frogfish and Boxer Crabs (*Lybia tesselata*).

Above: *Mandarinfish (Synchiropus splendidus) are one of the most colourful fish in the ocean. Always found amidst dead corals and only ever seen at dusk, the male performs an elaborate swimming 'dance' to attract females into a breeding zone, where they both dart together upwards from the reef expelling eggs and sperm.*

Lembeh Straits

Who would have thought that a 16-km (10-mile) stretch of fairly polluted water and dumping ground for most of northern Sulawesi's seaborne trash is actually the epicentre of muck diving. When the owners of Kungkungen Bay Resort first opened their eco-tourism dive lodge back in the 1980s, they decided to clean up the underwater rubbish that littered their home bay. However, they very quickly discovered that the trash was actually home to some of the most weird and wonderful underwater critters found on the planet.

Over 40 distinct dive sites are found here, all very different but all linked by a common theme: muck diving. Quite simply, by swimming along nice and slowly with your nose (and eyes) very close to the seabed you will soon spot some of the remarkable creatures that make Lembeh their home. They include Barramundi Cod (*Chromileptes altivelis*), Flashing File Clam (*Lima* spp.), nudibranchs too numerous to mention, as well as shrimps and crabs.

Jahir with its mini-wall is always a favourite on night dives for the number of species of shrimps and crabs which can be found. **Hairball** is favoured for its frogfish, Ribbon Eels (*Rhinomuraena quaesita*) and colourful dragonets. The **Police Pier** near Bitung harbour, is superb for tiny octopus, curious corals, slipper lobsters and large starfish which are preyed upon by Harlequin Shrimp (*Hymenocera picta*).

Above: Regarded as being on the endangered species list, Bangaii Cardinalfish (Pterapogon kauderni) are quite common in the Lembeh Straits, the result of a canny aquarium fish supplier releasing several fish into the wild to harvest at a later date. Juveniles tend to hang out in the spines of sea urchins and gradually make their way into staghorn corals as they mature.

Pulau Raja Ampat

Located in the western province formerly known as Irian Jaya, the part of West Papua governed by Indonesia, Pulau Raja Ampat or The Four Kings is an archipelago consisting of over 1,500 small coral islands, cayes and submerged reefs, as well as four fairly large volcanic islands covered in lush tropical rainforest. There are sheltered bays and lagoons, amazing muck diving and coral forests that defy description. The four main islands are Misool, Salawati, Batanta and Waigeo, and the smaller islands of Kofiau, Gag and Gam. It encompasses more than 40,000 sq km (14,445 sq miles) of land and sea and contains Cenderawasih Bay, the largest marine national park in Indonesia.

Now known worldwide as one of the most diverse and unspoiled areas on the planet, the locale is rarely visited. There are over 600 species of coral, 1,300 species of fish including (at the last count) 27 endemic species found nowhere else) and 700 mollusc species, creating quite possibly the richest coral reef ecosystem in the world. Incredibly, some 75 per cent of the species diversity of the planet is found here!

Around 20 km (12 miles) east of **Misool Island** are the limestone cliffs of Farondi. The cove at Goa Besar is just a riot of colour with sea squirts, leather corals, damselfish and chromis everywhere. Large Humphead Wrasse (*Cheilinus undulatus*) cruise past as you try to focus on radiant file clams, juvenile lobster and nudibranchs by the score. Large Ornate Ghost Pipefish hang out in the soft corals along with pipefish and curious spider crabs. One of the larger tunnels is huge at over 9 m (30 ft) wide and 18 m (60 ft) long with its entrances fringed by whip corals, beautiful soft corals and sea fans, all of which appear to have pygmy seahorses on them. At nearby **Verena's Garden**, the cavern opens up to an air space within the island completely enclosed from the outside world and illuminated by small shafts of light that penetrate from above.

Above: The fringing reef around the limestone islands starts at the surface and drops dramatically into the depths with a simply staggering amount of tropical fish, sponges and corals to be found.

Southern and Eastern Indonesia

Southern and Eastern Indonesia is widely known as Wallacea, named after
Alfred Russel Wallace who formed his theory of species' natural selection after
examining mammal and bird fauna in the region in the 1800s. Charles Darwin
supposedly was influenced by his theories and calculations and used them to
further his own career. Wallace's publications prompted Darwin to publish
his own work on the flora and fauna of the Galapagos. Wallacea excludes
New Guinea and the eastern Indonesia province of Irian Jaya. The islands of
Lombok, Komodo and Flores are also east of the Wallace Line.

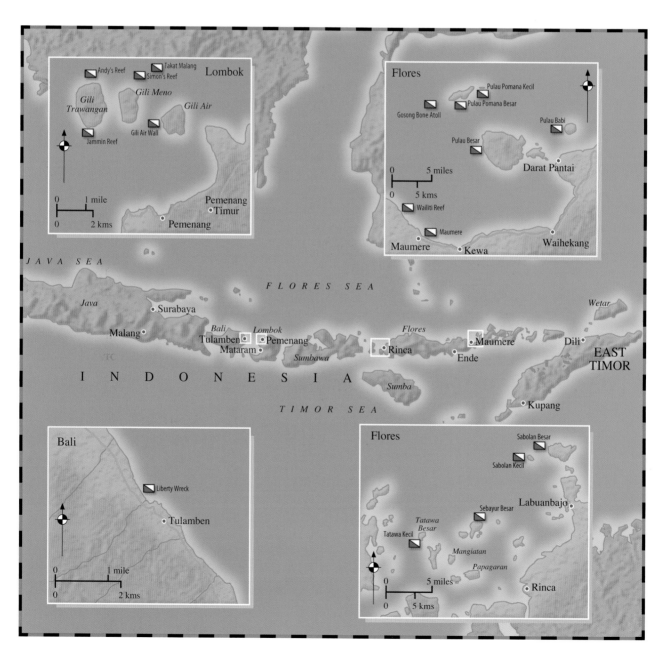

The USAT (United States Army Transport) *Liberty*, usually referred to as the ***Liberty* Wreck**, is undoubtedly one of the best wreck shore dives I have ever been on and it is suited to all levels of diver experience. Bali is an excellent diving destination with as much diversity of dive sites and marine life here as anywhere else in the region. This is the jewel in Bali's crown.

The *Liberty* served as a supply ship during the Second World War until she was torpedoed by the Japanese Submarine I-166 on 11 January 1942 while crossing the Lombok Straits. She was rescued and taken in tow towards Singaraja on Bali. The crew had to be evacuated and she was beached on the shore at Tulamben more than 70 km (44 miles) from the nearest safe harbour. The ship languished there for over 21 years until the massive and fatal eruption of the Gunung Agung volcano in 1963 pushed her over the wall and broke her back. Now the ship lies only 50 m (165 ft) out from the beach and has diving depths ranging from 5 m (16 ft) to 32 m (105 ft).

In the open aspects of the wreck there are Moorish Idols (*Zanclus cornutus*), angelfish, butterflyfish, lots of crinoids and feather starfish all with commensal Sea Urchin Shrimps (*Stegopontonia commensalis*) and tiny squat lobsters. The sea fans have Pygmy Seahorses (*Hippocampus bargibanti*) and Longnose Hawkfish (*Oxycirrhites typus*) and the hard corals are populated by Leaf Scorpionfish, frogfish, stonefish, gobies and blennies. There are schools of batfish, sweetlips, fusiliers, clouds of anthias to rival any coral reef scene and colourful nudibranchs and flatworms. There are cleaning stations everywhere with fish of all shapes and sizes queuing up to be cleaned by tiny wrasse and various shrimps. More than 400 species of fish and 200 species of nudibranch have been recorded on the shipwreck and beach!

Above: *A massive shoal of Bigeye Trevally (Caranx sexfasciatus) just to the seaward side of the wreck forms endless lazy spirals in the water column. Incredible.*

Lombok: Gili Islands

Off the northwest coast of Lombok are three small coral islands known as the Gili's. **Gili Trawangan** to the west is where most divers stay to venture out each day on the traditional wooden dive boats. The islands are surrounded by excellent coral reefs and the majority of dives are drift dives between the three islands. There is also a turtle sanctuary and divers can expect to see large numbers of them on every dive. **Andy's Reef** to the north is a mixture of sloping reef, vertical wall and buttress reef with patches of dead coral where dynamite fishing once took place. The drift dive to the south along **Jammin Reef** is exhilarating with good coral forests dotted along the sandy seabed in around 21 m (70 ft). There are sea snakes, large parrotfish, jacks and barracuda but few reef fish because of the strong current. **Gili Meno** has a good drift dive which takes you over an old concrete barge where huge frogfish can be found, but some of the best coral reef dives are to the east off the north coast of Gili Air. **Gili Air Wall** is better in shallower parts but the larger sea fans in 25 m (84 ft) have Pygmy Seahorses. **Simon's Reef** usually has very strong currents which scour through the mini seamounts which are topped with superb sea fans and crinoids. **Takat Malang** is another drift dive. There are some huge giant clams to be found here amid the swimthroughs, overhangs and coral bommies.

Above: Gili Trawangan is the most westerly of the three Gili's located off northwest Lombok. A turtle sanctuary, but known for its strong currents, the reefs are superb with expectations to see frogfish, Pygmy Seahorses, sea snakes and turtles, of course.

Flores

Flores is simply massive and therefore diving tends to be concentrated in either the western or eastern regions, unless you are using a live-aboard dive boat. The main town in western Flores is **Labuanbajo** and this has become the centre for most diving operations with travel times of around one to two hours to the western islands. To the west are a great selection of dives around **Tatawa Island**, **Sebayur Island** and the **Sabolan islands**. To the east are the superb reefs around **Pulau Besar**, **Gosong Bone Atoll**, **Pomana Islands** and **Babi Island**. **Sabolan Kecil** and **Sabolan Besar** each have a couple of dives with a maximum depth of around 30 m (100 ft) where the sloping reefs drop down to a sandy seabed. There are masses of coral species here and most are swarming with colourful basslets, anthias and damselfish, all of which just move gently out of the way as you swim by. The western side of the reef is more exposed and Manta Rays have been seen here. To the east, the reef is flat-topped and then slopes steeply down to the seabed. The top edge is favoured by snorkellers but is also a great place to hang out at the end of your dive as there is such good coral growth with huge table corals and brain corals.

Around Sabolan Besar the term 'tropical reef fish' is something of an understatement as there is just so much variety. There are large anemones with several species of clownfish on each one and they all have cleaning shrimps and porcelain crabs. It is a superb dive. **Tatawa Kecil** is tiny, just the tip of an undersea seamount. Again the maximum depth is only 30 m (100 ft) allowing you plenty of time to explore as you are always able to complete your safety stops in the shallows where the marine life is just as prolific. There are superb coral examples here as the entire area comes under the protection of the Komodo National Park.

Maumere is the main centre for diving in East Flores and the islands which dot the outer skirts of Maumere Bay are where the best diving is located. **Wailiti Reef** is located 5 km (3 miles) west of Maumere and divers usually make the 20-minute boat ride from Waira. This site is a small wall that drops down to the seabed at 20 m (66 ft). It is rich in soft corals, nudibranchs, tiny squat lobsters, shrimps, cuttlefish and famed for its Spanish Dancers (*Hexabranchus sanguineus*).

Below: Varied and colourful ascidians or sea squirts are symbolic of this region. As filter feeders they love the constant current which pushes through between the islands. Most areas of the upper reef, shipwrecks and other man-made structures are usually colonized by these colourful, yet delicate, invertebrates.

Pacific Ocean

The Pacific Ocean is by far the largest body of water on the planet. Covering over one third of the Earth's surface, it encompasses around 165 million sq km (64 million sq miles) and stretches from the Bering Sea in the Arctic to the Ross Sea in Antarctica.

There are many natural hazards in this tectonically active area: the Pacific Ocean is surrounded by 'the Ring of Fire', a region of active volcanoes and fault lines that have been responsible for terrible loss of human life through earthquakes, volcanic eruptions and tsunamis.

The western ocean floor is dominated by a staggering number of mountain peaks and ridges which support thousands of islands, coral reefs and atolls in the region known as Oceania. These are the focus for virtually all of the marine life found in the shallower seas. The majority of the world's diving occurs in these shallow waters between the Tropics of Cancer and Capricorn.

Above: Turtles are commonly seen on every dive, feeding on sponges and ascidians.

Left: Small schools of Oriental Sweetlips (Plectorhinchus vittatus) can be found facing into the current.

The Philippines

The Philippines comprise more than 7,100 islands and countless more coral islets and shoals, just waiting to be explored – the coastline is over 35,000 km (21,750 miles) long. The Philippines Trench to the east is one of the deepest troughs on the planet reaching 10,500 m (34,450 ft).

The country has 14 regions within four large island groups: Luzon and the capital Manila, the Visayas including Cebu, Mindanao and Palawan which has more than 1,700 islands in its province. After Indonesia, the Philippines is the world's second largest archipelago, yet more compact and much easier for inter-island transport.

As it is so close to the central hub of marine life in the Indo-Pacific, the biodiversity is incredible, but sadly over 70 per cent of the reefs have been damaged by destructive dynamite fishing, the commercial collection of corals and shells, and resort development entailing mangrove destruction. Despite these negatives, what is available for divers is stunning and easily comparable to what can be found in Malaysia and Indonesia.

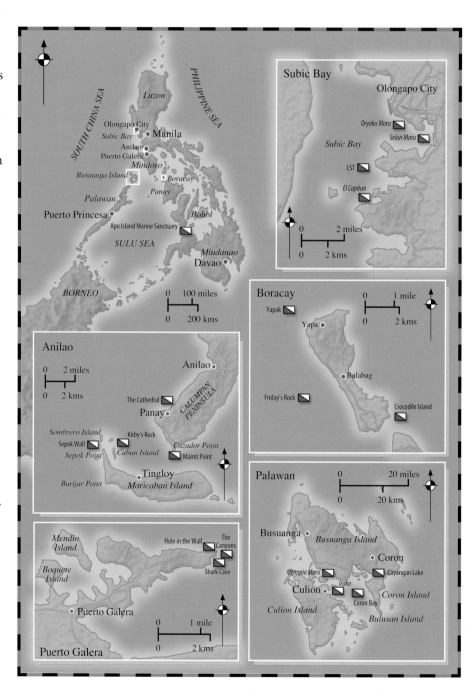

TRAVEL ADVISORY PHILIPPINES

Climate: The typhoon season lasts from around July to October, although in recent years it seems to have been starting and finishing later – in 2010, for example, there was severe flooding in North Luzon as late as November.

When to go: The best time is from the middle of December to the middle of May because that is off-season for typhoons. Any travellers to the country around Christmas or Easter are advised against travelling more than necessary as the entire country is on the move, making it difficult to get a seat on any type of transport.

Getting there: Getting to the Philippines is convenient as the country is well linked to the rest of the world. The major cities like Cebu and Manila act as the international gateways, and there are small internal flights to all the other islands, with easy transfers to resorts. This is a big country and you may spend more time travelling than you would like, but it is worth it!

Water temperature: Average annual temperature: 23–36° C (73–97° F). The visibility is not exceptional and averages from 6–21 m (20–70 ft).

Quality of marine life: Excellent, with a huge diversity of species, most of which will be common to the entire region.

Depth of dives: Averages around 15 m (50 ft) but most dives on the outer reefs will be much deeper.

Dive practicalities: Much of the diving is drift diving and the resorts all push the more experienced diving to encourage guests to see all the big pelagics, but the reef diving is excellent and should not be ignored. There are superb WWII shipwrecks around many of the islands, but invariably the visibility can be poor resulting in dark water.

Subic Bay

Previous page: *Clockwise from top left: colourful gorgonian sea fans are found on all dive sites; Clown Triggerfish (Balistoides conspicillum) are the most colourful and exotic of the species; tranquil bays and unhurried dive resorts are a speciality of the Philippines; good coral reefs and wrecks are situated just a short boat ride away from shore.*

Subic Bay, formerly an American naval base, is now open to recreational divers to explore the Second World War shipwrecks found there. The Bay suffers from poor visibility due to sedimentation but the half a dozen wrecks there are well worth exploring.

To the north of the airport runway is the *Oryoku Maru*, a Japanese troop transport and POW ship sunk in 1944, then subsequently blown up as it was a navigation hazard. This wreck is fairly flattened but the metal plates are now well encrusted and home to plenty of moray eels, sweetlips, chromis, hatchetfish and Glassy Sweepers (*Pempheris schomburgkii*). The former Japanese cargo vessel *Seiun Maru* was sunk in 1945 by the US Navy. The wreck is massive with huge holds and swimthroughs and is now well encrusted with coral, algae and sponge growth. Grouper, fusiliers and snapper are all over and in general it is in fairly good condition. At a depth of only 27 m (90 ft), it is good for exploring, although the visibility is often poor.

To the southeast of the runway and between Triboa Bay, Camaya Point and Grande Island two more ships are well worth exploring. There is an **LST** (Landing Ship, Tank) sunk in 1946. Although fairly low in profile, it is in 35 m (115 ft) and therefore deeper than some of the other wrecks. This restricts your bottom time as safety stops have to be made on this site. Completely open in aspect, the metal parts are all covered in corals, sponges, hydroids and tunicates and there are small schools of fish everywhere, being preyed upon by lionfish and scorpionfish. Batfish and fusiliers are usually in the water column and will follow you up the shotline as you make your safety stops.

The *El Capitan* was a small freighter and it lies in fairly shallow water on its port side. The best diving is around the stern as there is much more light. It has lots of lionfish, schools of chromis, fusiliers and snapper, small jacks are common and the ship's superstructure is completely covered with a complex web of hard corals, sponges and oysters.

Above: *The historic shipwrecks of Subic Bay and Coron Bay are in excellent condition but are subject to varied visibility. It is always better to take a dive light with you on all such dives.*

Anilao

Anilao or Batangas located to the south of Subic Bay has a large number of dive sites concentrated around the Calumpan Peninsula and Maricaban Island to its south. **The Cathedral** is regarded as one of the top dives in the region and is reached by dive boat just off Bagalangit Point. This Marine Park is very popular as the maximum depth is around 30 m (100 ft) and the fish are friendly.

Below: The reefs off Anilao have superb soft corals dotted all over, amidst colourful crinoids, sponges and ascidians. Current should be expected on most of these dives.

Cazador Point to the south has a dive site called **Mainit Point**. This is a very exposed site with plenty of current, so excellent for coral growth as you drop down the boulder mini-walls to 30 m (100 ft). Small schools of fish are always around but it is the brilliant blue of the small tunicates that attracts your attention.

Kirby's Rock off Caban Island between Calumpan and Maricaban has an easy coral slope to the shore but on the seaward side drops steeply to 18 m (60 ft) before sloping off to over 30 m (100 ft). Visibility is nearly always good here due to the tidal stream, which is never so strong that you cannot negotiate the site. The walls are covered with wonderful soft corals, small hard corals and sea whips. Most species of reef fish are found here and the site is superb for night dives as the cup corals come to life with brilliant colours.

Diving conditions on **Sepok Wall** at the northwestern point of Maricaban are usually fairly good with visibility around 30 m (100 ft). There is a very good coral garden in the shallows with Staghorn Corals (*Acropora formosa*), porites and brain corals everywhere. The wall starts at about 5 m (17 ft) and drops rapidly to around 27 m (90 ft). There are large sea fans, sea whips, soft corals, barrel sponges and cup corals.

Below: Anemone Porcelain Crabs (Neopetrolisthes oshimai) *are regularly found on most anemones. Impervious to their stinging cells, they hide amidst the tentacles and under the skirt, feeding on any waste products.*

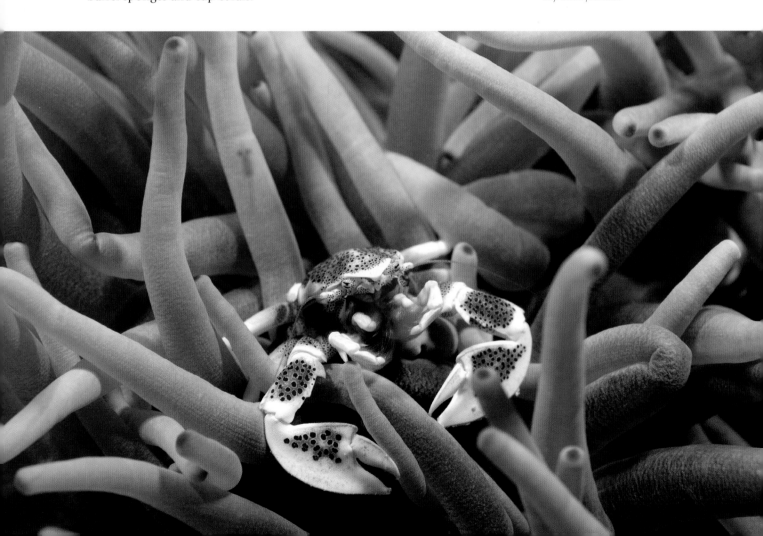

Mindoro

The island of Mindoro lies to the south of Luzon and tourists tend to favour the coastal strip on the eastern and northern part of the island where **Puerto Galera** (Port of Galleons) is located. Several well organized dive centres arrange their own transport for clients from Batangas on Luzon to Puerto Galera, thereby allowing divers that extra time on the island and in the water.

The two recommended sites are **The Canyons** and **Shark Cave**. I've also included **Hole in the Wall**, as this site is at the start of The Canyons and is much better for photographing reef life.

The Hole in the Wall has several stepped mini-walls from the coral plateau which is covered in large Table Corals (*Acropora clathrata*), topped with sponges and crinoids and these take you to the hole which is only about 1.5 m (5 ft) high. Fire Gobies (*Nemateleotris magnifica*) and Blue Ribbon Eel (*Rhinomuraena quaesita*) are found here as are frogfish, Ornate Ghost Pipefish (*Solenostomus paradoxus*) and Leaf Scorpionfish (*Taenianotus triacanthus*).

Above: Leaf Scorpionfish (Taenianotus triacanthus) are fairly common but difficult to find, due to their excellent camouflage, reflective eyes and ability to 'sway' in the current so resembling a leaf.

The Canyons are best dived on a strong flood tide when the visibility greatly improves, but the currents are not for novice divers. Starting at about 12 m (40 ft), the current sweeps you past the 'Hole in the Wall' cavern and will push you towards the canyon, where the depth drops to around 27 m (90 ft). The experienced dive guides will lead you towards an old Spanish anchor and then you are off again into the current and doing safety stops in open water. Even during the safety stops you will see emperorfish, batfish and possibly hammerhead sharks. Shark Cave to the east of Escarceo Point is an overhanging ledge at 29 m (97 ft) and is almost 30 m (100 ft) long. Whitetip Reef Shark (*Triaenodon obesus*) are always found under the ledge during the day. The dive returning back up the steep slope is excellent with very good coral growth, tons of fish and invertebrates.

The Visayas

The Visayas are the large central group of islands between Luzon and Mindanao and include six of the Philippines' major islands: Bohol, Cebu, Negros, Panay, Leyte and Samar.

Borocay is a small island to the north of Panay Island but is one of the top diving areas in the Visayas and has had an enviable reputation for over 40 years. There are dive centres and resorts all over Borocay and all have very high standards of equipment and dive expertise, particularly relating to some of the punishing currents, which can be found here. But not all diving is drift diving; there are great muck dives, shallow coral reefs and tons of colourful fish.

Yapak at the northern end of Boracay is really only suitable for experienced divers as the dive begins at 30 m (100 ft) and while depth is limited to 35 m (115 ft), the ocean depth exceeds 70 m (230 ft) here. Again principally a drift dive, as this is when the pelagics are best encountered including schools of tuna, trevally, Whitetip Reef Sharks, Spotted Eagle Rays (*Aetobatus narinari*) and much more!

Friday's Rock, on the other hand is suitable for all certification levels as the depth is 18 m (60 ft) with little or no current. Red snappers usually school over the rock as do fusiliers and small trevally. Covered in good corals, sponges and sea fans, there is plenty for everyone to enjoy.

Crocodile Island is about 15 minutes away from the main beach and suitable for all levels of diver. This site is arguably the most beautiful in Boracay due to the variety and colour of the soft corals and sea fans.

Five km (three miles) off the southwest point of Negros Island is the **Apo Island Marine Sanctuary** which can only be reached by boat from the North side of Dumaguete City. There are strict controls at this site with dive boats only allowed to moor onto the buoys available and a limit of 15 divers at any one time. Superb soft corals colour the whole area and the reef walls are filled with tropical fish, small spiny lobster, nudibranchs and shrimp. Don't forget to look out into the blue as you will see trevally, tuna, fusiliers, turtle, Whitetip and Blacktip Reef Sharks (*Carcharhinus melanopterus*), barracuda and a few rays.

Opposite above: Spider Crabs (Cyclocoeloma tuberculata) attach bits of algae, sponge and hydroids to their carapace and legs to help in their camouflage.

Above: Hairy Squat Lobsters (Lauriea siagiani) live on barrel sponges. It takes great patience to find them (usually with help from a dive guide familiar with the area).

Opposite below: Weird-shaped members of the lionfish family are Rhinopias which come in a variety of colour forms. Some are smooth-skinned, while others have complex attachments, fringes and fronds.

Palawan

Busuanga Island is the northernmost large island off northern Palawan; it has a natural bay and anchorage between Busuanga and Culion Island to its south called **Coron Bay**. Famous for the Japanese ships sunk there during the Second World War, there are over a dozen identified ships as well as numerous others awaiting identification. This exposed island is also home to some superb reef dives.

Southeast of Lusong Island and about a two-hour boat trip, one of the most popular wreck sites in Coron is the *Irako*, a Japanese refrigerated provision ship that was scuttled in 1944. At 145 m (476 ft) long she is still relatively intact and sits upright, listing slightly to port. Well encrusted with winged oysters, sponges, small soft and hard corals and lots of sea fans, she is a natural magnet for marine life including a couple of resident turtles, schools of jacks and barracuda and just about everything else in between. This is a deep dive at around 35 m (115 ft) and a maximum depth of 42 m (140 ft) so time is limited on the bottom.

The *Olympia Maru* is a former Japanese freighter sitting upright in approximately 27 m (90 ft) of water and located very close to Tangat Island. She is 122 m (400 ft) long and almost 17 m (56 ft) wide. With the shallower water and the upright position, you tend to average around 18 m (60 ft) on the dive, giving you good extended bottom time. It is an easy dive but a lot of the superstructure has shark-winged oysters and hydroids all over, so a full suit is advised for protection. This freighter is perfect for those who have done little wreck diving as she is so easy and safe (with guidance) to explore. Her holds are cavernous and there are usually several scorpionfish and lionfish around the edges of the ubiquitous Glassy Sweeper schools.

Cayangan Lake or Barracuda Lake as it is sometimes known is found around 30 m (100 ft) in from the north face of Coron Island. Midway between Limaa Point and Balolo Point, there is a gap in the cliffs at sea level. It is fairly easy to negotiate, but the rocks are sharp so it is best to wear strong footwear. The lake is calm and sheltered and surrounded by amazing limestone pinnacles. It has open channels into the sea and the water is always hazy as the hot water mixes with the cooler sea water. Nearer to the shore on the seaward side a number of marine fish can be found including snapper, squirrelfish and a big old barracuda which has been fed for a few years (not recommended!).

Above: Cayangan or Barracuda Lake is accessed along the north shore of Coron Island. Fed by underwater connections to the sea, it is only reached by a brisk walk across the rugged foreshore and cliffs.

Opposite: Colourful tunicates and crinoids colonize the superstructure of many of the wrecks of Coron Bay. The wrecks are now well broken up and deteriorating rapidly despite the colonization of so much marine life.

Melanesia and Micronesia

Melanesia and Micronesia are sub-regions of Oceania. The islands of Melanesia lie to the north and northeast of Australia and include Vanuatu, the Solomon Islands, Papua New Guinea and all of her satellite islands, the Maluku Islands, Norfolk Island, Rotuma, Schoutan Islands, Santa Cruz Islands, New Caledonia and the Torres Straits Islands. The Federated States of Micronesia lie north of Melanesia and comprise four island nations: Yap, Pohnpei, Kosrae and Chuuk (Truk). While the total land mass is relatively small at only 702 sq km (271 sq miles), the 607 islands occupy over 1.6 million sq km (618,000 sq miles) of the Pacific Ocean.

Opposite: Known worldwide for the quality of its soft and hard corals and super-abundance of fish, as well as its historic Second World War shipwrecks, this massive, diverse region is very popular with divers.

Below: Small but powerful dive boats are the order of the day when diving throughout Micronesia.

TRAVEL ADVISORY MELANESIA

Climate: Tropical year round. Hotter, more humid period with some severe tropical storms from November to April; cooler, drier time from May to October. Countries closer to the Equator (Solomon Islands) are generally hotter than those further south (Fiji, Vanuatu, New Caledonia). Average maximum temperatures vary from 22–28° C (72–82° F). Up to 400 cm (160 in) of rain can fall in the northern islands of Vanuatu annually.

When to go: The area can be dived all year round. May to October are usually best and the seas are calm, but sometimes suffer from periodic plankton blooms which can reduce visibility (but do increase the likelihood of large pelagic encounters). Whale-watching season (New Caledonia) is from July to September.

Getting there: Fiji: most international carriers fly from the USA, New Zealand, Japan and Australia. Solomon Islands: generally reached by air from Cairns or Brisbane in Australia, Auckland, New Zealand or Nadi, Fiji. Vanuatu: regular flights from Auckland, Fiji and Noumea. New Caledonia: international carriers fly from France, USA or Canada. Flights from UK go via Eastern Australia.

Water temperature: Average annual temperature: 25–30° C (77–86° F). The visibility can be excellent in many locations and will exceed 30 m (100 ft).

Quality of marine life: Fiji: known worldwide for the fabulous soft corals and amazing colourful walls. Solomon Islands: enviable reputation for the excellence of their marine life. Vanuatu: best known for its premier dive, the SS *President Coolidge*. New Caledonia: very high species diversity with many species not even named by science – yet.

Depth of dives: Averages over 18–30 m (60–100 ft) but most dives on the outer atoll reefs and on the wreck will take you into decompression if you are not careful.

Dive practicalities: Full suits are advised for protection against stinging hydroids and as it can be cool in the winter and windy on the surface in the returning dive boat. The water can be exceptionally clear, lulling you into thinking that you are much shallower than you actually are, so please pay attention to your computer or depth gauge.

TRAVEL ADVISORY MICRONESIA

Climate: Tropical, usually hot and humid all year round. Obviously cooler on the coast, with the Trade Winds blowing from November to May bringing lower humidity. Temperatures range between 26–32° C (80–90° F). Heavy rain can occur throughout the year, 280–1,016 cm (110–400 in) – 280 cm/110 in Yap and Chuuk to 1,016 cm/400 in in Pohnpei and Kosrae. Typhoons are rare although Yap was hit by a big typhoon in 2004 which caused widespread damage on land but the reefs fared better.

When to go: Palau: all year, but best from May to October when the seas are calmer; Chuuk: all year, as the lagoon is fairly sheltered; Yap: all year, but from November to May the Mantas are in Goofnuw Channel to the east and from June to October are found in Mi'l Channel to the northwest.

Getting there: International flights to Hawaii or Guam, then you rely on smaller aircraft and so there are more restrictions on baggage.

Water temperature: Averages 25–30° C (77–86° F). The visibility can be excellent in many locations and is usually between 12–30 m (40–100 ft).

Quality of marine life: Excellent, with more than 1,500 species of fish and 300 varieties of coral (Palau); shipwrecks covered in excellent coral and sponge growths (Chuuk); huge range of fish, corals and invertebrates but Mantas the real speciality, as there are around 100 which have made the plankton-rich channels and cleaning stations their home (Yap).

Depth of dives: Averages around 15–30 m (50–100 ft) but expect to go over 30 m (100 ft) when at the blue holes and out at reef wall dives (Palau/Yap); most dives on Chuuk will be shallower as some of the best wrecks are in quite shallow water.

Dive practicalities: The best diving is done by live-aboard dive boats which have all of the facilities you require, with staff to give expert advice and guided dives. Boat rides to the reefs can be rough at times, so take a full suit and some protection from the wind. The dive sites are usually calm and sheltered.

Palau

The Republic of **Palau** has a land mass of only 458 sq km (177 sq miles) and comprises eight main islands and a further 250 smaller ones and atolls. They constitute part of the Caroline Islands chain and are dramatically beautiful both above and below the waves.

The diving is world-renowned; the dives are as varied as the marine creatures that you are likely to find, with walls and drop-offs, coral gardens, blue holes, caves and caverns, Second World War shipwrecks and some amazing spectacles, such as the enormous giant clams and the saltwater jellyfish lake which has millions of stingless jellyfish that you can swim amongst.

Blue Corner off the western edge of Ngemelis Island is a fairly flat area of reef that starts around 13 m (43 ft) and juts out into the blue quite some distance before plunging into the depths. The sand gullies and patches are home to stingrays, sleeping nurse sharks, moray eels and large grouper. This area has plenty of shelter, but as you approach the outer edge, the current picks up and the big fish action here can be awesome. The current was so strong when the site was first dived that the dive masters invented the 'reef hook' which allows you to hook yourself onto the reef without causing any damage so that you can stay still in the water to enjoy the action as it swims past. Nearby are a series of four blue holes which are open from the top of the reef and join into a huge cavern that opens out onto the reef wall 33 m (110 ft) below.

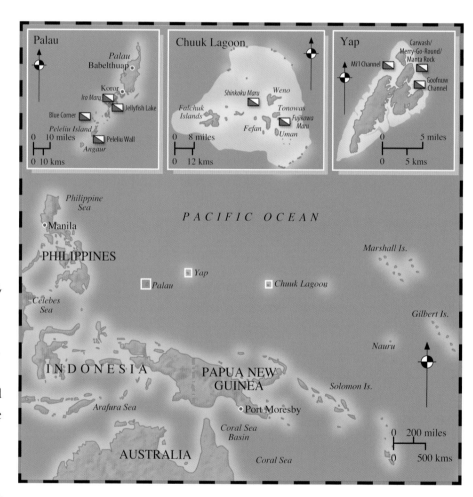

The **Peleliu Wall** off the southerly tip of the island of Peleliu is only reached by live-aboard dive boat. This is a really strong drift dive with the currents being so fierce that there is little coral growth on the top of the reef at around 9 m

(30 ft). But the reef wall is spectacular. There is some protection from the current in a large indentation in the reef wall; there are huge anemones and clownfish in this section as well as scorpionfish, lionfish and lizardfish.

Jellyfish Lake is reached by hiking high into the hills of Eil Malk island and then down the other side into a landlocked saltwater lake, surrounded by mangrove forest. There are several species of jellyfish here but they are not harmful as they no longer having stinging nematocysts in their tentacles. They feed off the algae that live within their bodies. The algae capture the sun's energy through photosynthesis and this is turned into food which the jellyfish can absorb. As the sun rises and sets each day, the jellyfish move back and forth across the lake allowing the algae to grow. At night, the jellyfish sink into the lower depths in the centre of the lake where the water is nitrogen-rich with heavy concentrations of hydrogen sulphide. This is only a snorkel dive, and is quite enthralling and a complete change from the majesty and colour of the surrounding reefs.

At the end of the Second World War, Palau actually had more shipwrecks than Chuuk, but many of the shallower ones were extensively salvaged and only the rough and jagged remains of the scrap are left. There are still many superb wrecks in deeper water which are hardly ever dived as divers are more interested in the coral gardens and walls. One of the top sites because of its sheltered conditions is the *Iro Maru*, located just a short distance from Koror.

Above: Jellyfish Lake is located on Eil Malk and while the hike is difficult, the reward of snorkelling amongst the thousands of stingless jellyfish that migrate across the lake each day is excellent.

Chuuk (Truk) Lagoon

Chuuk consists of 15 large islands, 192 outer islands and 80 islets. Located 993 km (617 miles) south of Guam, Chuuk is an enormous coral atoll featuring one of the largest lagoons in the world.

Due to its use as an operations centre by the Japanese in the Second World War, Chuuk was heavily bombed and is now a wreck diver's paradise, as the sheltered lagoon has very little current, reasonably good visibility and numerous shipwrecks in shallow enough water that they can be enjoyed by all levels of diver. One of the most popular is the *Shinkoku Maru* which is the second largest shipwreck in Chuuk at 152 m (500 ft) long. Sitting upright in 39 m (130 ft) of water the shallowest portions of her mast tops and bridge are only in 6–12 m (20–40 ft). Easy to penetrate, her bridge still contains her telegraph and guided dives will take you deeper into the interior. The marine growth is prolific and the fish life amazing. Thankfully, because she is in such a reasonable depth, divers can spend lots of time on her, decompressing slowly as they swim up the masts to the surface surrounded by schooling fish.

The *Fujikawa Maru* is probably the most famous of the wreck dives in Chuuk, principally because she is so shallow; her stern mast sticks out of the water and is intact. Lying in depths of 9–33m (30-110ft), this former cargo ship

Above: There are almost as many aircraft as there are shipwrecks in these waters, with several kinds found in Chuuk. Used as a Japanese naval base, it was heavily bombed as a reprisal against the Japanese attack on Pearl Harbor.

is 133 m (437 ft) in length. Her cavernous holds are stuffed full of military artefacts but the entire ship, in fact, is just an amazing site of soft and hard corals and sponges, with schools of fish visible at every part of the ship's superstructure and in the water column above.

Yap

Yap (pronounced *Wa'ab* by the locals) is one of four main islands and a further 14 coral atolls in the archipelago of the Caroline Islands.

The islands were formed as part of a huge plateau uplifted by the Philippines Sea Plate, with mainly rolling hills covered in verdant vegetation. They are surrounded by an extensive barrier reef encircling a beautiful lagoon next to the shore. Divers mainly come for the channels which cut into the lagoon from the outer reefs, as it is here that you can get up close and personal with giant Manta Rays (*Manta birostris*).

Above: It is easy to kneel on the sand and watch the graceful ballet of the Manta Rays as they come into the cleaning stations. Butterflyfish, angelfish and numerous wrasse species act as cleaners here.

The two locations are **Mi'l Channel** to the west and north of the main island and **Goofnuw Channel** to the east of Gagil-Tomil Island. Mi'l varies from 15–30 m (50–100 ft) deep, although it does drop off steeply outside the entrance of the channel. The main cleaning stations are found in the coral around 18 m (60 ft) deep, located on the north side of the main channel and known as Manta Ridge. Divers often start the dive in open ocean and drift into the lagoon, stopping at Manta Ridge on the way into the inner lagoon. Many just stay here but you can continue onwards to Manta Ray Bay further into the lagoon, where the current is much easier and wider.

Over to the east in Goofnuw Channel, the Valley of the Rays is a section of the channel about 15–20 m (50–65 ft) deep dotted with numerous low coral heads and bommies which are home to various cleaning stations. Other sites within the channel are **Carwash**, **Merry-Go-Round** and **Manta Rock**, all of which can be dived depending on the strength of the current at the time. All have cleaning stations and in general are treated as drift dives. Divers come for the rays but these same natural passageways into the internal reefs also bring schools of sharks and even Killer Whales (*Orcinus orca*).

Fiji

The Pacific nation of Fiji comprises some 800 volcanic and coral islands, of which 110 are permanently inhabited. The country covers some 3,000,000 sq km (1,000,000 sq miles) and is known as 'the Soft Coral Capital of the World'.

There are literally hundreds of coral atolls and you can track the evolution of a coral atoll from volcanic peak with a fringing reef all the way to the final stage of circular coral reef atoll and a shallow lagoon in the centre with no land at all: truly amazing.

Opposite: The Coral reefs and walls of Fiji are a riot of colour. Very similar in feel to the Red Sea in many places, there are superb, soft corals, anthias and fantastic vertical walls, caves and caverns.

Taveuni

In the northern province lies the island of **Taveuni** across the Somosoma Straits. Diving is done from live-aboard boats, principally around the northern reefs to the east around Qamea and Laucala and over the Somosoma Straits.

Sites such as **Stillwater** and **Bonnie's Boulder** are on the outer edges of an ancient atoll reef which was created when Qamea and Laucala gradually sank as the waters rose at the end of the last ice age. **Yellow Wall**, **The Edge** and **Noel's Wall** are all on a small atoll to the east. Misnamed, Stillwater actually has quite

strong currents around the tumbled reef system with depths of 6–24 m (20–80 ft). The old hard coral base was largely created by some devastating cyclones; however, the coral skeletons are now covered in fantastically coloured soft corals and sponges. Glassy Sweepers (*Pempheris schomburgkii*) swim in unison around predatory squirrelfish and lionfish and all the undersides of the ledges are festooned with Golden Cup Corals (*Tubastrea aurea*). Bonnie's Boulder is a large pinnacle surrounded by much smaller coral heads giving a good mix of both soft and hard corals as well as a great chance for pelagic encounters in the 'blue'. Depths are from 5–18 m (16–60 ft) and the site is as colourful for its fish as it is for corals.

Motualevu Atoll to the east has a spectacular vertical and often underhanging wall that drops way below safe recreational diving depths. Yellow Wall starts at around 5 m (17 ft) and there are all manner of soft and hard corals including sea whips, fans, black coral trees and golden soft corals by the

*Above: Blacktip Reef Sharks (*Carcharhinus melanopterus*) always patrol along the reef edge. Ignoring divers, they appear only vaguely curious about our presence.*

metre. The Edge has many anemones and their symbiotic associates, tons of colourful soft corals and also a vertical wall cut with small windows, arches and indented caverns just bursting with life and juvenile fish. Named after a nearby resort owner, Noel's Wall is known for its crystal-clear water and abundance of soft and hard corals, sponges, crinoids and fish that seem to tumble into the indigo blue of the abyss.

On the other side of the Somosoma Straits is a barrier reef off the south end of Vanua Levu known as the **Great White Wall**. 'Great' hardly does it justice as it is so much more than that. Dropping down the almost vertical wall, there is a negotiable cavern at 15 m (50 ft) that comes out onto a steep slope of white and light purple soft corals that stretch away before you. The overall colour is white, until you turn your dive lights on and this changes to lavender, dotted with brilliant splashes of red, blue and orange as other soft corals squeeze between them.

These are the few really good deep wall dives that Fiji has to offer and should not be missed during your visit to the islands.

Beqa Island

Approximately13 km (8 miles) south of Viti Levu and to the north of Kadavu is **Beqa** (pronounced Benga) **Island**. Beqa lagoon covers some 260 sq km (100 sq miles) and has a relatively stable water temperature all year round of 25° C (77° F). It is protected by 30 km (18 miles) of superb barrier reef on its southern and western edges and Beqa Island on the east, making for gentle currents. There is a great mixture of coral heads, pinnacles, coral gardens, vertical walls, fissures, canyons, caves and caverns, all covered in soft and hard corals and surrounded by plentiful fish. Couple that with the very good chance of seeing turtles and sharks and you the have the makings of a great diving area.

Found around 5 km (3 miles) from Pacific Harbour on mainland Viti Levu and 10 km (6 miles) from Beqa Island, **Caesar's Rocks** has been an incredibly popular dive site for many years now and it is obvious why. With a maximum

Above: Wherever the current becomes stronger on the more exposed headlands, gorgonian sea fans stretch out to snare the plankton. Crinoids and other filter feeders also hitch a ride to catch the particles in the current.

depth of only 18 m (60 ft), the ten larger coral bommies and other small coral outcrops are dominated by colourful soft corals interspaced with sea whips and gorgonian sea fans, all home to abundant tropical fish life. The bommies are all honeycombed with windows, tunnels and caves, with one in particular at 15 m (50 ft) that completely cuts through the coral head. The walls and entrances are covered with corals, bright yellow tunicates, white sponges, red sea whips and purple soft corals, a kaleidoscope of colourful reef life. Fish here are prolific, colourful and famously friendly, making it a great location for fish portraits.

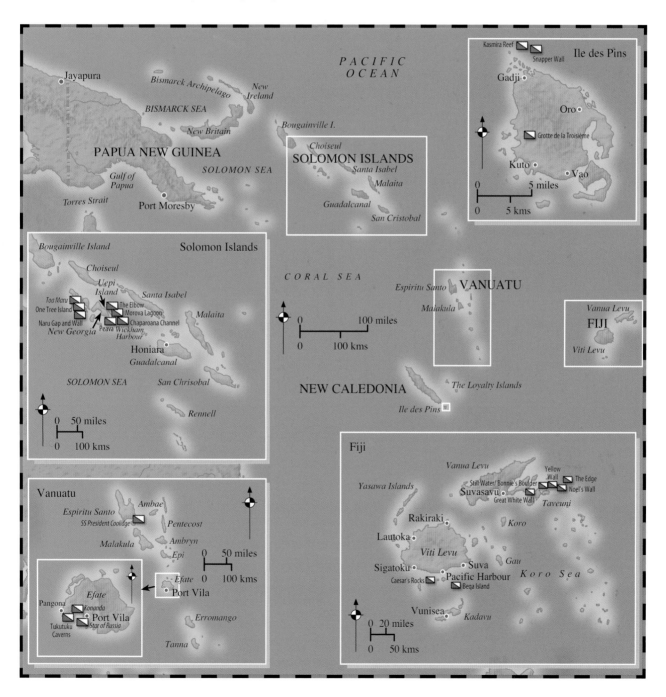

Solomon Islands

Located to the east of Papua New Guinea, there are over 1,000 islands in this group spread over 2,072,000 sq km (800,000 sq miles) of ocean. The capital, Honiara, is located on the island of Guadalcanal.

New Georgia

Morova Lagoon to the south of New Georgia is recognized by the World Wildlife Fund as being the largest island-protected saltwater lagoon on the planet. **Peava**, a lagoon within a lagoon, is well protected making it perfect for night diving and for finding many of the critters associated with muck diving.

The Bilikiki live-aboard dive boats visit the region frequently and offer superb diving on all of the best sites, including a few scattered shallow Second World War shipwrecks and aircraft. The deeper wrecks in Iron Bottom Sound are too deep for recreational diving. The diving around the outer fringing reef of Morova Lagoon offers walls that drop over 2,000 m (6,600 ft).

*Below: Whitetip Soldierfish (*Myripristis vittata) *congregate in the shallow caves and caverns during the day, waiting for darkness before they venture out onto the reef to feed on small fish and crustaceans.*

The island of **Uepi** is another popular choice and as there is only one resort on the island, it is usually fairly quiet and laid back. There are three wrecks in the **Wickam Harbour** area all of which are Japanese freighters sunk by aerial attack during the Second World War. With the seabed lying at only around 30 m (100 ft) here, the wrecks and their supporting ecosystems are easy to explore. The **Chaparoana Channel** which separates Uepi from its nearby neighbours is also a superb open water drift dive among swarms of pelagic fish. At a dive site called **The Elbow**, the vertical wall drops directly into the deepwater trench some 600 m (2,000 ft) below. The wall is cut with hundreds of caves, caverns, windows, tunnels and fissures all of which are covered with overhanging soft corals and sea fans. Turtles are usually seen on the ledges with their attendant remora suckerfish and lionfish patrol the edges of the small schools of Glassy Sweepers (*Pempheris schomburgkii*). While you do have to take notice of your depth limitations, most divers tend to stay around 12–15 m (40–50 ft) where there is the most light, colour and variety of marine life allowing you dives of around an hour each time.

Gizo

Gizo is a tiny island located in the Western Province where some of the major battles of the Second World War took place. There is an excellent choice of wreck and reef diving with depths between 6–40 m (20–130 ft). The best wreck is the *Toa Maru*, a Japanese transport ship over 135 m (450 ft) long. Now lying on her starboard side in Kololuka Bay in depths between 12–37 m (40–125 ft), she still has many artefacts on board and is now well encrusted with marine growth, with schools of fish all over the water column above. There are also a few fighter planes here, both American and Japanese. However, it is the marine life that comes out at night that makes this site special.

The **Naru Gap and Wall** at the entrance to Gizo Lagoon have very strong currents, but by 'going with the flow' into the shallower waters of the lagoon, you can swim alongside Mantas, sharks, schools of jacks, trevally and Dogtooth Tuna (*Gymnosarda unicolor*). The wall on the outside drops into the blue with excellent corals. **One Tree Island** resembles a stubby Bonsai tree on a bare rock; underwater the coral gardens in depths averaging 12 m (40 ft) are stunning.

Above: Denise's Pygmy Seahorses (Hippocampus denise) *prefer small gorgonian sea fans of a similar colour to help mask their presence. There are only a handful of pygmy seahorses discovered so far and all in recent years; they are all delightful.*

Vanuatu

The Republic of Vanuatu is a small Y-shaped archipelago consisting of 83 islands lying 1,750 km (1,100 miles) east of northern Australia. Now known for the TV reality shows that have been filmed here, it is still the magical reefs, wrecks and marine life that attract visitors to the islands.

While the emphasis here is on the wreck of **SS *President Coolidge***, there are also some very fine dives to be had around the southeastern shore of Espiritu Santo, within 30 minutes travel time by boat from Port Vila. Both reef and wreck dives, such as the ***Konanda*** and the ***Star of Russia*** are available for all levels of diving certification and all have good quality corals and fish life.

The **Tukutuku Caverns** are found about a 25-minute boat ride from Pangona, across the bay from the Vaughani Shores. There are literally dozens of well-lit, easy-to-explore caverns here, most of which are interlocked, creating delightful swimthroughs framed with delicate lace corals and Golden Cup Corals (*Tubastrea aurea*). Colourful sponges and brilliant red squirrelfish are found as are Whitetip Reef Sharks (*Triaenodon obesus*).

Above: Often used as a night dive, the Tukutuku Caverns really come to life with many different species of shrimp and nudibranchs.

The SS *President Coolidge*

The **SS *President Coolidge*** is known as the largest accessible shipwreck for recreational diving. She was a luxury cruiser before being requisitioned as a troop carrier during the Second World War.

She made several South Pacific runs and left on her last voyage to Espiritu Santo carrying 5,092 US officers and troops of the 172nd Regiment, 43rd Infantry division. On 26 October she came into the island, but had not been given any special warnings about the minefield there. She failed to stop in time and struck two mines. Almost all the troops on board managed to escape after the captain ordered her to be beached. Shortly after, she slipped down over the reef and rolled over onto her port side with her full cargo of munitions still on board.

Below: Most divers recognize the SS President Coolidge only from the carving of the Lady and the Unicorn, but many divers are quite content not to attempt the deep penetration and just enjoy the ship's colourful, coral encrusted exterior.

Due to the physical size of the wreck and the depth of the water, there are now at least 20 different dives to be had. Sitting from 18–60 m (60–200 ft), this is quite a formidable site, but is easily reached as most divers just go in off the shore, swim down the marker line and start their tour from the sharply pointed bows. Visibility is usually around 15 m (50 ft) making it ideal even for beginner divers to enjoy the exterior of the ship.

The ship is slowly rusting and rotting away but because of its strong construction, it can be penetrated with a guide. The obvious highlight is the statue of the Lady and Unicorn at the end of the First Class smoking room in 35 m (120 ft). This is a long deep dive and only those with the experience of deep dives and good buoyancy should consider it.

Deeper down the ship is the First Class swimming pool, still with its mosaic tiles, the other pool was removed for access into the holds by the War Department. Much of the ship is open and light streams through into the dining rooms and corridors, where moray eels, trumpetfish and batfish reside. This dive should be treated as a night dive at all times, to allow you to see into the farther reaches of the ship and make the absolute most of your opportunity on this amazing old ship.

New Caledonia

New Caledonia is a sprawling archipelago located 1,500 km (930 miles) east of Australia and 1,700 km (1,050 miles) north of New Zealand.

Unlike other nearby islands which are much more volcanic in origin, New Caledonia is part of an ancient continent which has been drifting across the planet for the last 250 million years. Because of its oceanic isolation, three-quarters of 3,500 species of plants are endemic. There are more than 1,000 species of fish recorded and over 6,500 types of invertebrate found in the shallow coastal lagoons, atolls and coral walls. New Caledonia has one of the largest coral lagoons in the world which covers 24,000 sq km (9,300 sq miles) and includes a 1,600-km (1,000-mile) long barrier reef.

The New Caledonian Authorities have created marine reserves on several islets to protect the marine life. However, there are two large nickel-mining operations on the island and the water run-off has quite clearly killed corals with silt and other pollutants, creating very real concern for the marine life. Offshore sites such as the Ile des Pins and the main lagoon around the Belep Archipelago are much better, with clearer waters, more species diversity and no endangered sites.

Above: New Caledonia has one of the largest coral lagoons in the world and the entrances into the lagoon are home to large numbers of sharks, snapper, jacks, barracuda and batfish.

Ile des Pins

Sometimes referred to as the **Devil's Grotto**, the Grotte de la Troisième is a superb cave dive on the west coast of the **Ile des Pins** (Isle of Pines) with an average depth of only 6 m (20 ft). The entrance to the caves is partly hidden by trees and bushes on the cliffs and is only accessible by jeep over a rough track that cuts into the rainforest. You then have to climb down around 90 m (300 ft) along a rather rough path into the cavern with all of your equipment to reach this freshwater pool. Visibility is usually superb at over 30 m (100 ft) and with the light cascading in from above, the orange and white stalactites and stalagmites are simply stunning. There are a few side passageways and openings into other grottos but there is very little else to see except to enjoy the scenic wonder of a cavern system that was once on dry land.

Off the northern shore of the Ile des Pins, **Kasmira Reef** has a depth of around 16 m (54 ft) before the seabed slopes gently away into the blue. There are small caves, caverns and tunnels in the reef, all of which are full of soft and hard corals, the occasional sleeping nurse shark as well as plenty of snapper and surgeonfish. There are rays in the sand as well as shrimp gobies, Fire Gobies (*Nemateleotris magnifica*), colourful anemones and clownfish, schools of blue fusiliers, flying gurnards and trumpetfish.

Nearby is **Snapper Wall** also located about a 20-minute boat ride from Vao. This is a leisurely drift dive along the edge of the reef; there are large schools of snapper, as well as jacks, fusiliers and surgeonfish. The shallower parts of the reef around 12 m (40 ft) have sergeant majors, chromis and various wrasse and parrotfish species.

Above: Only coming out at night, curiously shaped Coral Spider Crabs (Hoplophrys oatesii) can be spotted on their host species of soft coral, where they attach parts of the soft coral to their shells for camouflage.

Papua New Guinea

Known officially as the Independent State of Papua New Guinea (PNG), the country occupies the eastern half of the island of New Guinea. It is one of the most culturally diverse countries on the planet and has over 800 different local languages. Part of the British Commonwealth, PNG gained its independence from Australia in 1975.

The country is vast and includes the islands of New Britain and Bougainville, and the Bismarck Archipelago. The most northerly point is the uninhabited island of Sae, to the south is Tagula island and the eastern borders join with Irian Jaya, the easternmost province of Indonesia. There are over 6,000 islands around its shores and evidence has been found that the island was populated more than 50,000 years ago.

The earliest divers were those involved in pearl fishing around Milne Bay. It was not until the 1960s that sport diving started to become popular, but the country is so vast and the dive sites so special that there are still very few divers on her reefs and wrecks, making them some of the most pristine dive sites in the world. There are over 40,000 sq km (15,450 sq miles) of coral reefs with virtually no commercial fishing. Estimates consider that PNG is home to over twice as many species as the Red Sea and over five times as many as the Caribbean.

Opposite: Clockwise from top left: Anemone crabs are found on most anemones vying for space with anemonefish and shrimps; Golden Cup Corals (Tubastrea aurea) only come out at night. They are a relation of the anemone; whip corals are host to several species of goby and small shrimp; the coral reefs are incredibly colourful and pristine.

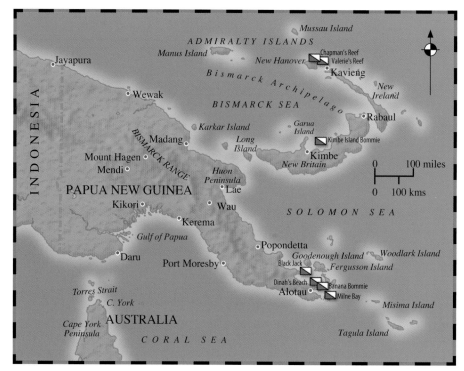

TRAVEL ADVISORY PAPUA NEW GUINEA

Climate: The climate is tropical but very varied as the area is so vast. When it is the dry season in Port Moresby, it is the wet season in Milne Bay just next door (so to speak). The southeast Trade Winds blow from May to November, but all the diving areas have sheltered bays and inlets, even on the more exposed offshore islands.

When to go: The area can be dived all year round, with November to February bringing the very best diving conditions and May to September bringing the heaviest rainfall.

Getting there: Getting to PNG is easy as most international carriers link through Australia, Japan and Hong Kong into Port Moresby. The local airline Air Nuigini links with most international operators and allows for transfers to the tourist areas and resorts.

Water temperature: Average annual temperature: 25–30° C (77–86° F); the visibility can be excellent in many locations and will exceed 30 m (100 ft).

Quality of marine life: Excellent, with a spectacular range of fish and critters. The term 'muck diving' was first coined here and the region is known for its staggering diversity of species, some of which are still new to science and have not been named.

Depth of dives: Averages around 15 m (50 ft) but most dives on the outer reefs will be much deeper.

Dive practicalities: Full suits are advised as there is just so much life around the reefs and wrecks including microscopic stinging things, so it is best to cover up. When snorkelling, always wear a shirt as the sun is relentless.

Milne Bay

Located in the southeast corner of PNG, **Milne Bay** has more than 435 named islands. It has brilliant muck diving but is also known for a terrible battle during the Second World War and the seabed is littered with the relics of that conflict. To the west of Milne Bay to Cape Vogel is the superb natural anchorage of Basilaki Bay and a dive site known as **Black Jack**. It is here that one of the world's best preserved aircraft wrecks can be found lying in 27 m (90 ft) of water. Sitting upright and intact, this large four-engined Boeing B-17 bomber is now home to several anemones and clownfish, crocodilefish, sweetlips, great soft corals and sponges. There are rarities found here too, including Hairy Ghost Pipefish (*Solenostomus* spp.) and jawfish. A superb dive.

To the north of Milne Bay are several good dive sites, such as **Banana Bommie** which is hidden just below the surface. Rising from 30 m (100 ft), it is best to dive the site with the current passing the west face as the marine life and drifting fish are awesome! Crinoids tip most of the table corals and the barer patches of sub-reef are home to sea cucumbers, nudibranchs and many species of shrimp and crabs. **Dinah's Beach** nearby is the original muck diving site, similar to Lembeh but without the trash, this shallow dark volcanic sand slope is stuffed full of fascinating species such as Mimic Octopus (*Thaumoctopus mimicus*), frogfish, seahorses and weird varieties of scorpionfish.

Below: This hermit crab has made its home in the beautiful shell of a Horse Velute (Fusinus undatus) sea snail.

Kimbe Bay

Kimbe Bay is found on the northern side of New Britain Island. There are several coral pinnacles in the bay which have profuse marine life, superb forests of gorgonian sea fans and are frequented by whales, including Killer Whales (*Orcinus orca*), and dolphins. **Kimbe Island** is 46 km (25 miles) north of Walindi and can be a difficult dive due to its exposed position. It is prone to strong winds and currents. With superb shallow reefs where you can spend your time off-gassing, most divers come for the wall that plunges way over 50 m (165 ft) as it is here that you will be rewarded with large groups of fish and several species of shark which cruise the waters.

Closer to Walindi and only 22 km (12 miles) north is the small island of **Garua** and its several small satellite islands. Much of the immediate diving from Walindi is done around here as the maximum depth is only around 30 m (100 ft). You can stay as shallow as you want as great critter encounters can be found all the way into the shallows. There are small Blue-spotted Rays (*Dasyatis kuhlii*), sand anemones with porcelain crabs and several species of clownfish, sand divers, razorfish, dragonets, gurnards, garden eels, triggerfish and many different species of shrimp-gobies. On the coral walls in deeper water are gorgonians, soft corals and sponges full of hawkfish, basslets, parrotfish, angelfish, butterflyfish and wrasse.

Above: Steinitz's Shrimp Goby (Amblyeleotris steinitzi) and its attendant shrimp have a very close relationship. The shrimp is nearly blind and depends on the fish for warnings of danger, while the shrimp excavates the burrow for the goby to hide in.

Bismarck Archipelago: New Ireland

Kavieng is the provincial capital of New Ireland and to the west is the island of Lavongai (New Hanover). Cut by several straits and passes between the innumerable islands lying between the two are some punishing currents, but these bring superb nutrient-rich waters which wash this maze of islands and provide the backdrop for stunning diving in crystal-clear waters and a profusion of marine life. It is the Kavieng region that is known best for its pelagic encounters, particularly with schools of eagle rays, large grouper and sharks. More suitable for experienced divers, again the emphasis here is on BIG things but it is the little critters which make us just as happy!

Chapman's Reef south of Ao Island near Cape Matanalem starts from the mooring line at 10 m (30 ft). It is a ridge reef that runs parallel to the shore with a very steep drop-off at its eastern end. Not for the faint-hearted, divers are usually dropped in off the reef and allow the current to bring them in close. Reef hooks are worth having but most divers just enjoy the drift with large schools of trevally, barracuda, emperorfish, batfish, surgeonfish, unicornfish and, of course, the sharks. The fish life amid the corals is really good too and most divers only get to appreciate this part at the end of the dive as they decompress slowly coming up the shoulder of the reef ridge. A slightly easier dive is known as Chapman's #2 where the current is not as strong and the reef comes up to around 5 m (17 ft). You can still expect to see turtles, sharks and eagle rays, but the reef here is superb with beautiful gorgonians and soft corals. The reef structure is also interesting with a separate coral bommie at one end that is teeming with small tropical fish life, crinoids and starfish.

Above: Frogfish are always a delight to find. Here supported on a finger sponge, this Ocellate Frogfish (Halophryne ocellatus) waits for unwary fish to come close enough to eat.

Off the northwest side of the East Islands and north of Taskul on New Hanover, **Valerie's Reef** is another dive for experienced divers. These offshore reefs fringe the coast and rise from the depths to around 10 m (33 ft). Most are uncharted, but they have become world renowned for the encounters with Silvertip Sharks (*Carcharhinus albimarginatus*).

Opposite below: Undulate Moray Eels (Gymnothorax undulatus) *hunt amidst the folds and convolutions of large barrel sponges where they hope to find small fish and crustaceans.*

French Polynesia

Covering an area of the southern Pacific Ocean as large as Europe, French Polynesia conjures up an exotic image. Places like Tahiti, Moorea, Bora Bora and Rangiroa are legendary symbols of beautiful lush green islands and lonely atolls where black pearls are harvested.

There are actually five archipelagos. At the extreme north are the Marquesas; the low-lying Tuamotus are found to the west and comprise some of the finest coral atolls in the world; the Gambier Archipelago to the east is more rugged but has even more atolls; to the southwest the Society Islands are perhaps the most scenically beautiful; and the Austral Archipelago lies to the south, with a more temperate environment, cooler waters and poorer visibility. But Rurutu is one of the very few locations on the planet where you can swim with Humpback Whales (*Megaptera novaeangliae*) – astounding!

Diving also includes some incredibly rich reef and wall dives, dazzling wrecks and a myriad of bejewelled tropical fish, corals and other invertebrates. For novice or first-time divers, there are superb shallow-water dives on sites that are akin to diving in an aquarium.

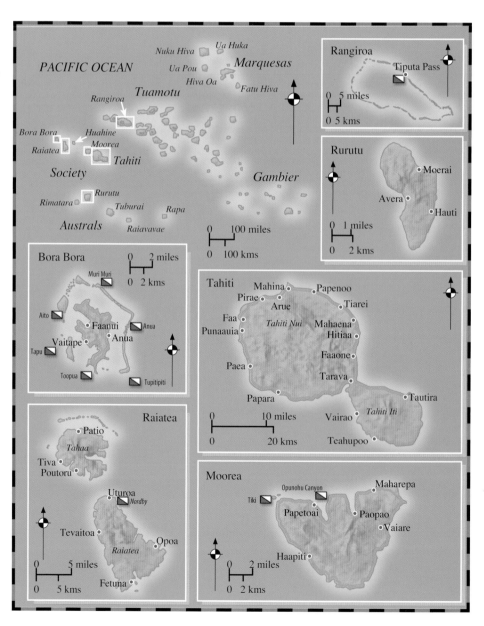

TRAVEL ADVISORY FRENCH POLYNESIA

Climate: Tropical and usually hot and humid all year round. Obviously cooler on the coast, with the Trade Winds blowing from November to May offering lower humidity. The average year-round temperature is 27° C (81° F).

When to go: Scuba diving is good all year round. The best diving conditions are between April and November; late August to late November for whale watching on Rurutu. The experience is always magical!

Getting there: International flights to Tahiti. Air Tahiti provides four 45-minute flights each day from Papeete, the capital, to Bora Bora.

Water temperature: Local visibility often reaches 40 m (130 ft). The average temperature of the ocean is 26° C (79° F). There is no noticeable temperature variation between the surface and a depth of 50 m (160 ft).

Quality of marine life: Excellent, with a super range of fish, corals and invertebrates, but really it is the whales, Mantas, sharks and exciting drift diving that most come for.

Depth of dives: Averages around 25 m (80 ft) but most dives on the outer reefs will be much deeper.

Dive practicalities: Most of the diving is fairly easy, but there are some punishing currents in the passes on some islands. Water temperature does drop in the south and while thicker wetsuits are recommended, especially while snorkelling with the whales, many divers opt for the lighter wetsuit or lycra suits.

Bora Bora

Bora Bora is the quintessential tropical island surrounded by a coral reef lagoon, gorgeous above and below the sea. Here tourists are usually either honeymooners in search of (and finding) a tropical paradise, or scuba divers who come for the possibility of Manta Ray (*Manta birostris*) encounters in the inner lagoon.

However, there are a number of other dives to be had including **Aito** which is a drift dive on the outside of the lagoon reef; **Tapu**, another ocean dive but this time with great shark encounters; **Muri Muri**, also known as **White Valley**, has sharks, as well as dolphins and barracuda; **Tupitipiti** is a steep wall that drops over 75 m (250 ft). The top lagoon dives are **Anua** for the Manta Rays and **Toopua**, which is famed for its eagle rays, caverns, tunnels and swimthroughs.

Anua off Fitiu on the eastern side of the island has depths of between 3–25 m (10–80 ft). This inner part of the lagoon is also popular with snorkellers as the Manta Rays use the shallow sandy pass in their patrols of the plankton-rich currents which sweep through the lagoon. Best between May to December the Mantas are there every day and will vie for your attention with huge Napoleon Wrasse (*Cheilinus undulatus*), large snapper, grouper and moray eels.

Above: Common dolphins are seen regularly at the entrances of the lagoon passes.

Opposite above: Divers off Tahiti Nui will expect to be accompanied by several Blacktip Reef Sharks (Carcharhinus melanopterus) for the entire dive.

Opposite below: Bicolor Angelfish (Centropyge bicolor) are shy in nature but soon become accustomed to the photographer's presence.

Tahiti

There are some excellent dives on **Tahiti Nui** and its adjoining smaller island of **Tahiti Iti**. The vertical gorgonian walls are superb but it can be difficult to concentrate on the nudibranchs, clams, shrimps and tropical fish when there are several Blacktip Reef Sharks (*Carcharhinus melanopterus*) keeping you company. Huge Napoleon Wrasse and schools of parrotfish and tangs graze the reef top.

On the main island of Tahiti Nui, the western wall of Tahiti is excellent, with plenty of fish, good quality corals and quite breathtaking in its scope. The wrecks are of a 30-year-old wooden supply ship and a vintage World War II Catalina seaplane, both of which are located near the airport runway in the sheltered inner lagoon.

Moorea

Moorea is just a short ferry ride west of Tahiti. Most of the corals in the shallows under 18 m (60 ft) are rather poor but it is the sharks for which divers come. The inner lagoon is not nearly as developed as that on other islands and the pass from the outer reef also has more manageable currents. The outer reefs are fairly good with large numbers of barracuda, snapper, surgeonfish, unicornfish and Blacktip Reef Sharks patrolling the reef edge. There are always plenty of tropical reef fish darting in and out of the coral ledges.

Shark feeding at the **Tiki** and **Opunohu Canyon** dive sites is popular with Grey Reef Sharks (*Carcharhinus amblyrhynchos*), Blacktip Reef Sharks and Lemon Sharks (*Negaprion brevirostris*) being the predominant species. While this looks a bit uncontrolled, the sharks appear well used to the whole thing and overall it can be quite a thrilling experience.

Rurutu

More temperate in climate, this small island has cooler waters and less visibility than the northern islands and atolls, but it is around **Rurutu** that you can swim with Humpback Whales (*Megaptera novaeangliae*). From late August to late November, female Humpbacks visit the safe waters of Rurutu to give birth and mate. Accompanied by one or two mature males, who are most favoured for mating, and several juvenile opportunistic males (some things never change!), the females congregate in the shallow waters near the reef passes.

The local boats, piloted by fishermen, are licensed to carry six passengers and a guide to minimize the stress to the whales. Once a breaching whale is sighted, the boats move to the approximate area while the whale goes through its regular breathing routine of surfacing approximately three times before 'sounding' or diving deep on the fourth breath. This behaviour is quite obvious, as it is the only time that the whale lifts its gigantic tail clear of the water. Once the whale sounds, it can be around 15 to 18 minutes before it returns to the surface to breathe, during which time the whale is having a short rest or sleeping.

Above: *Whale watching is big business in Polynesia and when the Humpback Whales (Megaptera novaeangliae) arrive in Rurutu around August to November each year to calve and mate, the local fishermen take tourists out under licence. Topside encounters include breaching, tail and fluke slapping, sounding and general boisterous behaviour.*

The best encounters are with a resting or sleeping whale, as they tend to be suspended in around 15–25 m (50–80 ft). It is at this point, when the whale almost reaches the surface, that you are allowed a shallow snorkel dive and the chance to photograph these mighty beasts. In-water encounters are never guaranteed and the underwater swimming can be very crowded but there are numerous sightings on the surface to be enjoyed.

Above: Snorkellers are allowed into the water when the whale comes to the surface to breathe. However, there is never any guarantee that you will be able to have any interaction.

Rangiroa Atoll

Top of the list for many divers is a visit to one of the largest atolls in the world. At over 75 km (50 miles) across, **Rangiroa** is more like an inland sea. It is surrounded by tiny islets or *motu*, for the most part uninhabited, save for the thousands of seabirds that have found sanctuary there. On either side can be found the two channels that feed and cleanse the lagoon twice daily. In particular, **Tiputa Pass** to the east is incredible. Once the location of a former river, when Rangiroa used to be a mountain millennia ago, it has depths on the ocean-side of the pass of over 70 m (230 ft), rising to 6 m (20 ft) on the inside of the cut.

The reef wall at the easterly side is where the action is. There are hundreds of Grey Reef Sharks accompanying the divers and swirling masses of barracuda overhead. Underneath are untold numbers of red Bigeye Snapper (*Lutjanus lutjanus*), Moorish Idols (*Zanclus cornutus*), butterflyfish and jacks. At least half a dozen turtles chomp happily at the sponges and soft corals, oblivious to the frantic attacks by threatened clownfish and damsel fish.

Opposite: To 'feel' the sound of the singing male Humpback Whale reverberating in your chest is the experience that will always be remembered. It is only the males which sing and the song changes yearly.

Raiatea

Over on **Raiatea**, reef, drift dives and shark encounters are also the norm but there is also the best wreck dive in French Polynesia. Actually a shore dive in front of the Hawaiki Nui Pearl Beach Resort, just south of the island's capital Utoroa, the *Nordby* lies in around 25 m (80 ft). This ship lay forgotten for more than 100 years before the Hemisphere Sub Club De Plongée, run by Hubert Clot, opened his doors at the hotel. Imagine his surprise when this former iron barque was discovered lying on her port side along the edge of the house reef. Originally christened the *Glenearn* and built in Dundee in 1873, she was sailing under the Danish flag when she sank during a sudden violent storm in 1900. A superb night dive, the hulk is covered with *Tubastrea* cup corals, colourful nudibranchs and clams.

Above: Sunk in 1990 off the coast of Raiatea, the wreck of the Nordby is a superb shore dive. Although the visibility is reduced due to the nearby river, nevertheless it is home to an amazing number of species of invertebrate.

Eastern Australia

astern Australia comprises Queensland, Victoria and New South Wales. Great diving can be had all along the east coast, but it is the tropical diving destinations in the north that are explored here.

Dominated by the Great Barrier Reef, which hosts the largest number of marine life organisms on the planet, it has some 600 continental islands including their fringing reefs, more than 300 coral islands or keys, 2,900 individual coral reefs including hundreds of atolls all set in an area covering 350,000 sq km (135,000 sq miles). It has approximately 1,500 species of fish, 4,000 species of mollusc, 350 types of reef-building hard corals and over 400 different varieties of sponge. Countless thousands of other invertebrates, crustaceans, worms, soft corals, nudibranchs, anemones, sea squirts and jellyfish are found as well as squid, cuttlefish and octopus. Migrating whales, dolphins, Dugong (*Dugong dugon*) and turtles also ply these waters, making them irresistible to divers and naturalists.

Divers visit to enjoy the experience of scuba diving and snorkelling on the largest barrier coral reef system on the planet. Many opt for the live-aboard dive option to check out some of the uncharted sites. However, most of the dives are operated close to the main tourist centres by day boats which run out to the nearest reef systems.

Opposite: Clockwise from top left: Colourful sea fans are synonymous with the outer walls of the northern Barrier Reef; due to its massive size, the Great Barrier Reef is visible from space; sea snakes are regarded as very venomous but they rarely approach too close to divers; the coral fields of the northern Barrier Reef as it extends into the Coral Sea are pristine.

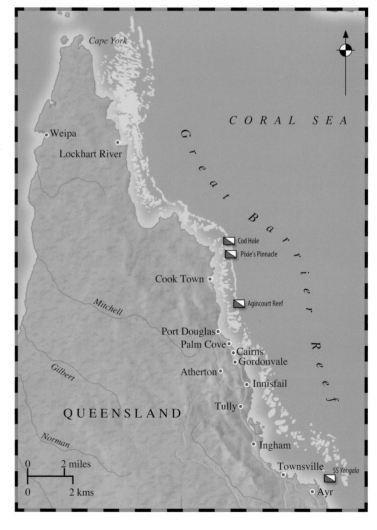

TRAVEL ADVISORY EASTERN AUSTRALIA

Climate: Due to its length, there are significant seasonal differences in the weather pattern. There is a distinct wet season in the north from December to March. Humidity is also very high in the north, but much better once you get onto a live-aboard dive boat. The region is regarded as being tropical in the north with land temperatures varying from 26–30° C (79–86° F).

When to go: The prevailing southeasterlies blow from April to October, but virtually all of the reefs are protected on the lee shore. Wetter from December to March, this is also a great time for sightings of Whale Sharks and migrating whales.

Getting there: Flights to Cairns, Port Douglas and Townsville are regular and easy. Most international carriers fly directly into Cairns. Live-aboard dive boats are the best option for divers and Mike Ball has one of the best operations in the Coral Sea.

Water temperature: Averages 24–30° C (75-86° F) throughout the year but dropping to 20–28° C (68-82° F) in the south with visibility averaging around 25 m (80 ft)

Quality of marine life: Very good overall with a great representation of most marine tropical fish and invertebrates, plus huge friendly Potato Cod!

Depth of dives: Averages around 25 m (80 ft) but most dives on the outer reefs will be much deeper. The *Yongala* is in less than 30 m (100 ft) and most of the best accessible reefs are in shallow water with great snorkelling being a nice alternative.

Dive practicalities: The diving is fairly easy overall, but due to the high concentrations of microscopic marine life in the water and the box jellyfish (a deadly venomous cnidarian invertebrate which is found around November to March), it is always better to wear a full suit for protection.

Great Barrier Reef

Visible from space, the Great Barrier Reef lies just off the coast of eastern and northeastern Australia, and is recognized as one of the true Seven Wonders of the World. This reef is a labyrinth of small lagoons and reefs widely spread out and it covers some 2,000 km (1,250 miles) of ocean. It is the largest biological ecosystem on the planet.

Pixie's Pinnacle

West of the true Barrier Reef, most divers tend to concentrate around the main tourist areas of Townsville, Cairns and Port Douglas. One such site is the popular tourist dive of **Pixie's Pinnacle** located on No.9 Ribbon Reef. This single large coral head rises from 37 m (125 ft) to within 1 m (3 ft) of the surface. It is cone-shaped and has a flat top which is over 15 m (50 ft) across. While this is regarded as a novice or snorkel dive (and more often than not this little coral pinnacle is the first of many experiences that visitors have of the Barrier Reef), the bommies have a great representation of all the marine families that are found on the Barrier Reef. At night this little pinnacle just lights up with *Tubastrea* Golden Cup Corals and colourful soft corals all 'hopping' with brilliantly coloured shrimps, small spider crabs and nudibranchs. Snails in colourful shells venture out onto the reef which has crinoids and basket stars everywhere.

This is just a 'taster' of what is to come. Many go on to **Agincourt Reef** located on Ribbon Reef No.10. Again, many tourist dive boats visit the reef and your dives will be dependent on your qualifications, ranging from the simple shallow coral heads (or bommies) to the superb Blue Wonder which has a vertical wall that drops beyond 40 m (130 ft).

Above: Pairs of Coleman's Shrimp (Periclimenes colemani) enjoy life on the top of a stinging sea urchin where they snip off some of the spines to make it more comfortable for them.

Cod Hole

To the north of Ribbon Reef No.10 is the renowned **Cod Hole**. At only 20 m (65 ft) deep it is perfect for all levels of diver who want to get up close and personal with some giant Potato Cod (*Epinephelus tukula*) which can grow to over 2 m (6½ ft). Discovered back in 1973, this is probably one of the most famous dives on the Barrier Reef and one that every diver wants to experience. As always, it is only when you swim away from the main arena that you will start to appreciate the true beauty of this part of the Barrier Reef.

Above: Cod Hole is one of the more famous dives on the Barrier Reef. Large Potato Cod (Epinephelus tukula) have had many years of fun, at our expense, being fed and petted. While the feeding no longer happens (most of the time!), they still appear to enjoy the interaction.

The SS *Yongala*

Much further to the south lies the wreck of the passenger and general freight ship, the **SS *Yongala*** which is now fully protected under the Historic Shipwrecks Act. She was originally built in England and launched in April 1903. Her main operations were based along the Queensland Coast. She left Mackay on what was to be her final voyage on 23 March 1911 but, unknown to her captain, she was heading into a cyclone. Sadly she never showed up and her 122 passengers and crew simply vanished. It wasn't until 1958 that the wreck was discovered.

Visited by over 10,000 divers each year, she is now regarded as one of the top ten shipwrecks to dive in the world. She lies on her starboard side and is 109 m (358 ft) long. Her top port railing is at only 12 m (40 ft). Soft corals and sea fans predominate with small hard corals, sponges, hydroids, clams and winged oysters. The ship is simply surrounded by schools of fish with kingfish, trevally, barracuda, fusiliers, chromis, anthias, wrasse and jacks everywhere, as well as large Napoleon Wrasse (*Cheilinus undulatus*), grouper, stingrays, marbled rays, batfish, a resident Hawksbill Turtle (*Eretmochelys imbricata*) with its shell covered in red and green algae, olive sea snakes, wobbegong sharks and even the occasional guitar shark and Whale Shark (*Rhincodon typus*), as they all pass through the channel where the wreck is situated following the plankton as it passes through the Great Barrier Reef.

Below: The SS Yongala was lost in a storm in 1911 with all hands and passengers. However, she wasn't discovered until 1958. Now on everyone's diving list when visiting the Barrier Reef, it is recognized as one of the top wreck dives in the world. Although you have to accept staying on the exterior, there is everything from the tiniest invertebrate to the largest cetacean to be found here.

Caribbean Sea

The name **Caribbean** describes the horseshoe-shaped ring of islands, over 3,200 km (2,000 miles) long, separating the **Gulf of Mexico** and the **Caribbean Sea** to the west and south from the great expanse of the **Atlantic** to the east. Within this ring of island nations are four huge coral atolls, a further 7,000 islands, islets, submerged reefs, atolls and cayes organized into 30 territories covering 2,718,200 sq km (1,049,500 sq miles). The Caribbean Sea also hosts the largest barrier reef in the northern hemisphere and the second and third largest barrier reefs in the world.

There are vast migrating schools of fish and cetaceans as well as breeding grounds for turtles, whales and dolphins, spectacular coral reefs and more shipwrecks than anywhere else. Only 10 per cent of Spain's treasure fleet made it back home and this treasure bankrolled the country for over 300 years, leaving a legacy that, for the most part, is still lying spread over the entire Caribbean basin.

Above: Beautiful Azure Vase Sponges (Callyspongia plicifera) *are a common site.*

Left: *Typically, the Caribbean Sea has incredibly clear water.*

Bahamas

The islands of the Bahamas sit astride the Tropic of Cancer and are situated only 30 minutes flying time from Florida. From a tourism point of view, the Bahamas shot to fame because of the James Bond movies, as most of the underwater action was filmed around the islands. In fact, all of the wrecks used as props can still be dived around Nassau, while some of the cavern locations are south in the Exuma chain.

The Bahamas are regarded as one of the top diving locations in the world and certainly the number one spot to get guaranteed action with sharks. The Bahamas consist of over 700 islands and 2,500 small cayes (pronounced keys), and lie scattered across more than 160,000 sq km (100,000 sq miles) of ocean.

The larger islands of New Providence, Andros and Grand Bahama are home to some of the most varied scuba diving in the Caribbean. However, it is the smaller islands to the south which provide some of the best diving that the region has to offer. This attracts more experienced divers who enjoy vertical walls, challenging drift dives and even encounters with larger mammals, such as migrating Humpback Whales (*Megaptera novaeangliae*) from December through February. Because of the parallel formation of the reefs and the close proximity of each of the dive sites, the dive types are split up into three different depth ranges to suit different standards of diver. Most diving is done as a twin-tank dive in the morning and a single-tank dive in the afternoon.

Opposite: Clockwise from top left: Theo's Wreck is a favourite dive off Grand Bahama Island; the Bahamas are known worldwide for the hundreds of blue holes that are found all over their realm; technical divers are able to explore some of the deeper fissures in the blue holes of Andros; the Exuma Cays stretch south amidst shallow sandbars and incredibly coloured shallow seas.

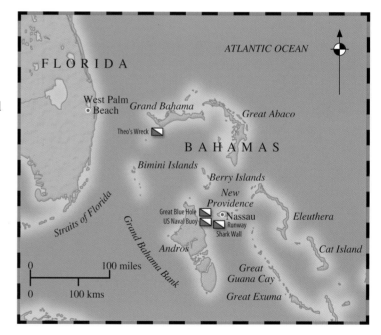

TRAVEL ADVISORY BAHAMAS

Climate: Tropical maritime climate with nice warm winds and cooler breezes next to the shore. Largely influenced by the weather patterns of North America in January to March, it can be quite cool dropping to 15° C (60° F). Care should be taken from June to November as this is hurricane season, with most of the rain also falling in that period. In summer, temperatures can rise to 40° C (104° F) in the southern islands and with a high percentage of humidity, it can get very sticky!

When to go: All-year-round. All of the islands have lee shores and good diving can be found on all of them. Caribbean Reef Sharks can be seen all year.

Getting there: Nassau on New Providence Island is the capital of the Bahamas and the international airport is located there. Nassau has direct flights from most of Europe and the United States. A few small air companies also fly to the Exumas and Bimini, but most inter-island flights all connect through Nassau first.

Water temperature: There is a wide fluctuation of temperature as the Bahamas are fed by the Gulf Stream, yet are also influenced by the cooler Atlantic waters. It ranges from 17–28° C (63–82° F). Visibility is usually around 25–30 m (80–100 ft).

Quality of marine life: The Bahamas have a typical selection of Caribbean marine life, and great experience is to be had with sharks.

Depth of dives: Averages around 25 m (80 ft) but most diving will be done as a twin-tank dive with a deep dive to 30 m (100 ft) first, followed an hour later by a dive to around 18 m (60 ft). Afternoon dives and night dives are generally above 12 m (40 ft) max.

Dive practicalities: Diving is generally easy in the Bahamas, but there are also dives to test your skill, such as deep caverns, shipwrecks and drift dives. It can be as easy or difficult as you want to make it. Full suits are required as a thermal barrier in the winter months.

Great Blue Hole

The **Great Blue Hole** to the east of North Andros is particularly well known and can be accessed by boat from both Andros and New Providence Island. It is over 90 m (300 ft) across; its outer rim starts at a depth of 14 m (45 ft) and drops to the centre at around 25 m (80 ft). On entering the water, the outer coral plateau is covered in small sea fans and sponges, but as you drop over the edge into the blue hole, you enter a gloomy world of sulphurous green-tinged water. You can even smell this sulphur underwater, through your face mask!

These fissures drop way below safe diving depth, but the water becomes much clearer, the deeper you go. Three levels of the hole can be visited. Level one is at the top of the shafts adjacent to the main fracture; level two is at 42 m (140 ft) where you can drop down a large hole into a tunnel where the bottom is at 98 m (320 ft). Level three is really only for very experienced cave divers as this involves diving around the perimeter at 58 m (190 ft) rising up through a narrow constriction at 33 m (110 ft) to safety above. Reef sharks and barracuda tend to hang out in the shallower waters, particularly where the visibility is poorest. The full scale of this spectacular dive can only be appreciated if you snorkel it first.

Above: *Blue holes are gigantic circular depressions in the limestone matrix which lead to spectacular undersea caverns filled with stalactites and stalagmites.*

Shark Rodeo

Possibly the greatest variety of shark encounters will be found south of Nassau, the capital of the Bahamas on New Providence Island. Here at Stuart Cove's Dive South Ocean, there is controlled feeding, but the excitement is particularly intense when you first enter the water as part of a two-tank dive trip to the **Shark Wall** and **Runway**, where there are two distinct types of shark dive.

The first dive is always an open-water experience in deep water, swimming with the sharks along the lip of the oceanic trench which drops 1,800 m (6,000 ft). Here there are at least a dozen resident Caribbean Reef Sharks (*Carcharhinus perezi*) and several large grouper which will accompany you on your dive (curiously lacking in other fish!). On the second dive, the shark feeder leads you a short way in from the lip of the wall into a wide sandy natural amphitheatre. Here, dressed in either a full chain-mail suit or a minimum of chain-mail sleeves and gauntlets, the sharks are fed by means of a blunt pole-spear, extracting commercially caught fish scraps from a large container.

The Bahamas are viewed as the number one shark diving destination after lengthy habitualization to humans of large numbers of primarily Caribbean Reef Sharks. There are also dives with Tiger Sharks (*Galeocerdo cuvier*), Blacktip Reef Sharks (*Carcharhinus melanopterus*) and Silky Sharks (*Carcharhinus falciformis*). However, there are also splendid wall dives – the edge of the continental shelf starts in quite shallow water here.

Below: Off Bimini in the north-west, a small group of Great Hammerhead Sharks (Sphyrna mokarran) are found in shallow waters, just a short distance from the shore and seemingly easily approachable with the aid of bait fish scattered on the seabed.

US Naval Buoy

Located out in the centre of the Tongue of the Ocean, 13 km (8 miles) southwest between New Providence Island and Andros Island, one of the more exciting dives is under the **United States Naval Buoy** or D.N.M. (Deployed Noise & Measurement Buoy), which is used for submarine tracking and exercises by NATO. The buoy is anchored to the seabed in 1,800 m (6,000 ft) of water. The attraction of the dive is not only the deep water and open ocean experience, but also the very high probability of encountering pelagic Silky Sharks. The naval buoy is 6 m (20 ft) in diameter and the flat underside has become overgrown with algae that attract small pelagic fish. Small organisms land there during the planktonic stages of their lives and are further preyed upon by larger and larger fish until the sharks show up. The sharks are also attracted by the vibrations of the attachment cable as the current passes through this natural deepwater trench.

Above: The US Naval Buoy is one of the most exciting open-water diving locations in the world. Where else can you swim over a deep ocean trench and catch Silky Sharks by the tail!

It was by chance that Stuart Cove saw the potential here for one of the most exhilarating diving experiences in the world. After lengthy discussions with the commercial and sports fishing organizations in the Bahamas, as well as individual sports fishermen, shark experts and conservation groups, an agreement was finally made that long-line fishing would be prohibited around the buoy and that any sharks caught by sports fishermen would be set free.

However, some Silky Sharks now had hooks, barbs and lures protruding from their jaws, obviously causing them discomfort and in some cases proving a real hindrance to feeding and or putting them in serious danger of dying. Stuart had learned of a harmless way to immobilize the sharks, called 'tonic immobility'.

If you grab hold of the tip of the shark's tail and bend it over, the shark immediately becomes dull, unresponsive and almost catatonic for between 30 to 90 seconds. This was enough time to free the hooks from the sharks' mouths and then release them, with relatively little hazard posed to the catcher. The problem was: how do you catch the shark? Easy, just bait the water, attract the sharks to feed in front of you and when one gets close enough, grab it by the tail (to remove those fishing hooks)! Surprisingly enough, the scheme worked.

Theo's Wreck

Built in Norway in 1954, the MV *Island Cement* had completed her working life and was due to be scrapped; her engineer Theodopolis Galanoupoulos suggested that she should be sunk as a diving attraction off Grand Bahama Island. With the help of the Underwater Explorers Society (UNEXSO) 'Theo's Wreck' was finally sunk in 1982 just off the Silver Beach Inlet.

Resting on her port side the 70-m (230-ft) long ship has a maximum depth of 33 m (110 ft) under her stern. The shaded areas above her rudder and propeller are covered in Golden Cup Corals (*Tubastraea coccinea*) and brilliant red sponges, as is the underside of her bow. Completely open in aspect, you can swim into her interior and along the railings and even into the main bridge compartment. She is completely covered by soft corals, small stubby hard corals and huge rope sponges. Large green moray eels hide in pipes, juvenile Spotted Drum (*Equetus punctatus*) do their gyrating dance under some metal parts, Queen Angelfish (*Holacanthus ciliaris*) and French Angelfish (*Pomacanthus paru*) swim by in their life-long pairs and chromis, Creole Wrasse (*Clepticus parrae*) and fusiliers fill the water column. At night, the wreck really comes alive with colour, as torchlight illuminates all of the colourful cup corals and sponges.

*Above: A resident pair of huge Rainbow Parrotfish (*Scarus guacamaia*) rest on the superstructure near the bow and small shrimp and lobster creep out into the open among basket starfish and crinoids.*

Mexico

Protruding like a giant thumb from the east coast of Mexico, the Yucatán peninsula is a huge land mass which divides the Gulf of Mexico from the Caribbean Sea. The most well established resort area is the purpose-built enclave of Cancun on its northern tip. This fascinating peninsula is mostly low-lying, covered by dense jungle and swamps criss-crossed with rivers, and scattered about with the intriguing ruins of the great Mayan civilization. As well as being rich in history, the Yucatán is also blessed with superb beaches lapped by the crystal-clear waters of the western Caribbean, sophisticated resorts and some of the best diving and snorkelling in the Caribbean.

Offshore from Cancun are three islands, the largest of which is the world famous diving destination of Cozumel. Her sister islands are Isla Mujeres and Isla Contoy which lie to the north. These three islands in the western reaches of the nutrient-rich Gulf Stream are formed in part by the largest barrier reef in the northern hemisphere, which stretches north from Honduras, Guatemala and Belize.

Above sea level, the land is rather uninspiring and the coral platform of Cozumel is all that is left of the tip of an ancient volcano. The immediate surprise is the exceptional quality of the diving down the coastline, where, in addition to the virgin reefs offshore, there is also the added bonus of exciting and challenging cave diving in the spectacular cenotes, or limestone sink-holes. You will very quickly appreciate that the diving to be found here is world class.

Both Cancun and the coastline to the south suffer from the periodic winter storms which occur in the southern Caribbean, resulting in a long low swell which makes boat trips and times between dives rather uncomfortable. This is where diving in the cenote really comes into its own.

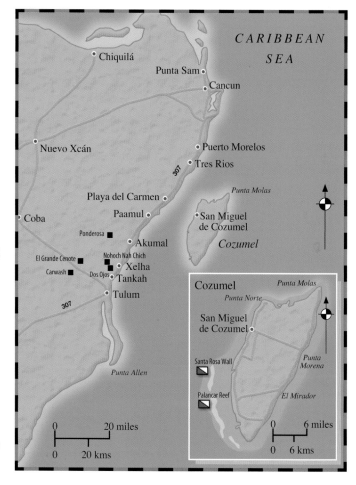

TRAVEL ADVISORY CARIBBEAN MEXICO

Climate: Tropical maritime, with nice warm winds, but also very high humidity. June to November is hurricane season, with most of the rain also falling in that period. In summer, temperatures can rise to 40° C (104° F).

When to go: November to March is best for the freshwater dive sites as there is always a high algae bloom in the summer, rendering visibility like 'pea soup'! May to September is considered best for the Cozumel reefs, but this is also hurricane season.

Getting there: Cancun and Cozumel are directly accessible from a number of airport hubs in the USA. Cancun is a great base to travel down the Mayan Riviera to the cenote and it is easy to catch one of the regular ferries to Cozumel to save flying.

Water temperature: Does not vary much and averages around 28° C (82° F). Visibility is usually around 18–30 m (60–100 ft) and considerably more in the cenote.

Quality of marine life: Fish life is exceptionally varied and the largest concentrations are found surprisingly in Cancun Bay. There are some of the largest schools of snapper and grunt I have seen anywhere in the Caribbean. There are one or two interesting fish to look out for, or should I say 'listen out for'. Toadfish in particular are worth mentioning. The name comes from the curious loud 'croaking' which you can hear quite clearly underwater. They live under a hollow of coral which seems to magnify the sound and it can carry quite far underwater. It certainly helps you locate them, as they are only active at night.

Depth of dives: Averages around 25 m (80 ft) but most diving will be done as a twin-tank dive with a deep dive to 30 m (100 ft) first, followed an hour later by a dive to around 18 m (60 ft). Afternoon dives and night dives are generally above 12 m (40 ft) max.

Dive practicalities: Virtually all of the diving in Cozumel is drift diving, so divers must be very aware of their buoyancy at all times. Always take extra sunscreen to plaster on after the dive as boat trips can take as long as one hour to the more distant dive sites. You must wear a protective suit and hood at all times as the freshwater temperature in the cenotes is about 10 degrees cooler than the sea and the freshwater mollies and tetras can bite quite painfully.

Cozumel

Cozumel is Mexico's largest Caribbean island at 47 km (29 miles) long by 15 km (9 miles) wide. *The Island of Swallows*, as it was once known, is ranked by the American diving press in the top five destinations for Caribbean diving with good consistent water clarity of over 30 m (100 ft) on average. This also means it is one of the busiest.

Although the onboard dive masters will plan your dive and dive time, it is pretty haphazard and they always lean towards the most inexperienced diver, cutting down your own bottom time. Therefore it is very important to do your own pre-dive planning.

Palancar Reef is one of those names which is always mentioned when divers talk of Cozumel. The reef is simply massive and of the 150 dive sites registered around Cozumel, Palancar has four. Stretching over 5 km (3 miles), this largely pristine reef offers an amazing diversity of marine life and coral formations to suit all tastes and levels of diving expertise. As all of your diving will be drift diving, there is little diver intrusion on the reefs which are well fed from the nutrient-rich waters of the Gulf Stream.

Further to the north is the **Santa Rosa Wall** and this is perhaps one of the favourite dives in Cozumel. In fact this reef can easily be split up into three totally separate dives giving much better opportunities to see its bounties. As in any exposed area, the southernmost section is low-lying and scoured by currents. The middle section has some very large tunnels which completely cut through the reef crest and the most northerly area of reef has tunnels, caves, overhangs and some very steep sections of wall running to near vertical conditions.

Above: Cozumel is well known for its drift diving, brilliant corals and superb large sponge growths.

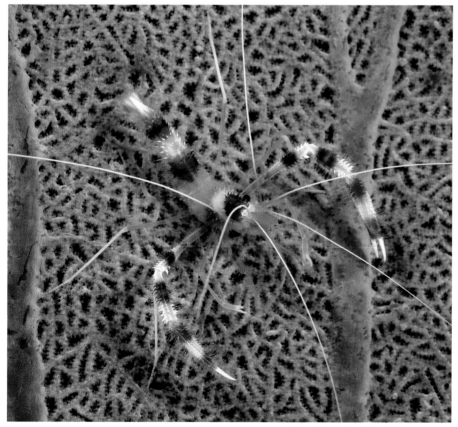

Above: *Nassau Grouper (*Epinephelus striatus*) are a common, large and friendly grouper found on all reefs. They are becoming the main predators of the invasive lionfish.*

Left: *Banded Coral Shrimps (*Stenopus hispidus*) are as happy on a sea fan as they are in a hidden nook in the reef. They act as 'cleaners' to many species of reef fish.*

Cenotes

South from Cancun on the Highway Mex 307 past Puerto Aventuras towards Akumal and Tulum you will come across signposts for cenote diving. More than 250 million years ago the entire Central American Continent was underwater and during the last ice age the sea level dropped and ultimately left a shallow raised plateau of soft porous limestone. This bedrock is susceptible to erosion and severe tropical rainstorms over the centuries have created huge underground caverns and wells. A cenote is created when the roof of one of these vast caverns collapses. In the south of the country, near Chetumal, is Cenote Azul, the deepest cenote in the world at over 100 m (330 ft).

There is a charge for all cenote diving as it takes place on private land – some have crude changing huts or simple platforms at the water's edge. Although **Nohoch Nah Chich** is the most famous, other sites such as **Ponderosa**, **Dos Ojos** and **Carwash** are easily accessible, but for sheer scale **El Grande Cenote** is absolutely superb. This huge circular hole is a collapsed cavern over 60 m (200 ft) across with the centre completely filled in. Entry is 6 m (20 ft) down a set of rickety steps to the edge of the cenote where you will dive into the labyrinth of inter-connecting caverns only lit occasionally by shafts of sunlight coming through other cenote entrances. The entrance to the cenote has a carpet of lily pads.

Gauging visibility is always difficult, but when you are more than 60 m (200 ft) into the cavern and you can see someone snorkelling at the entrance, you know it is good! There are stalactites, stalagmites, flow stone and many other fabulous formations.

Opposite: Freshwater lilies can be found at the entrance to many of the cenotes. Often overlooked as divers go past to explore the many underground caverns, they make a colourful backdrop to the dive.

Above: The entrance to the Carwash cenote is quite small but quickly slopes down underwater. Various piles of branches and leaves can be found at the entrance reducing the visibility but it gets much clearer as you descend.

Cuba

Cuba is the largest island nation in the Caribbean and is located in the Greater Antilles group of islands. It is situated at the entrance to the Gulf of Mexico and consists of the main island of Cuba, the Isla de la Juventud (Isle of Youth) and many small archipelagos covering 110,922 sq km (42,830 sq miles).

Cuba gained formal independence in 1902 and in 1959 Fidel Castro ousted Fulgencio Batista's dictatorship. While still estranged from the United States, Cuba is now open again to serious tourism. Huge investment in the infrastructure is ongoing yet evidence of the Cuban Revolution is found everywhere and what better way to find out about the country than in one of the many vintage American cars, all of which date back to before the revolution.

The reefs, walls and shipwrecks to be explored offer some of the best diving in the Caribbean. All the diving is done by small boat going out on either a single-tank dive each time or for an extended twin-tank dive, with the exception of Los Jardines de la Reina (Gardens of the Queen) where the diving is done from a live-aboard as the area is simply vast.

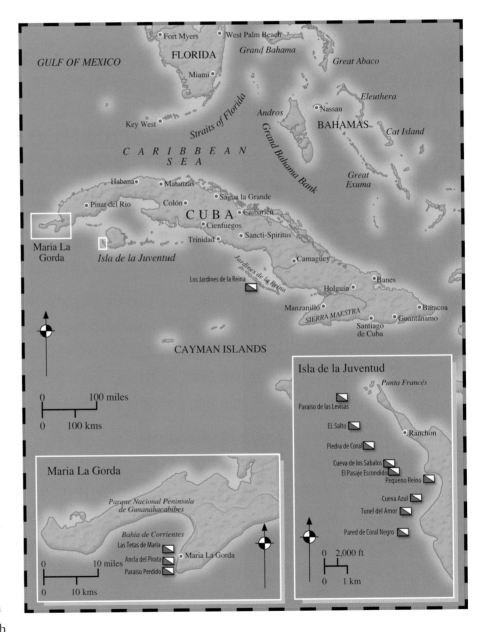

TRAVEL ADVISORY CUBA

Climate: November to April is the dry season, May to October the rainy season with the east coast more subject to hurricanes from August to November.

When to go: The best time to go is between December and April, when there are fewer tourists and better weather conditions, although prices will be higher then. Peak times for tourists are often the uncomfortably hot months of July and August. In theory, diving is possible all year round, as the island is large enough to make a plan should one region be 'blown-out'.

Getting there: The island is well connected throughout the Caribbean and beyond. (New cruise ship terminals are being built, the airport is expanding and hotels are rising at a rapid rate in anticipation of the relaxation of the US sanctions.) Virtually every other country has direct international flights into Cuba.

Water temperature: From around 22° C (72° F) in December to 29° C (84° F) in July. Visibility is usually around 25–30 m (80–100 ft).

Quality of marine life: Coral formations are all very good with a plentiful supply of fish because commercial centres have been concentrated in small areas, allowing little or no pollution or development construction to affect the coastline and mangrove forests. The coastline is fed by the Gulf Stream bringing plankton-rich waters to feed the 50 species of hard corals, 200 species of sponge and countless invertebrates and fish.

Depth of dives: Averages around 25 m (80 ft). Some of the wall dives can be much deeper, but depths are usually restricted to 30 m (100 ft) for safety reasons.

Dive practicalities: Diving is varied and often very extreme with some strong currents near the offshore pinnacles. Be careful when relaxing on the beach, as both the sand flies and the very hot sun can be ferocious. You should wear a full 5-mm wetsuit in the colder months, including a hood, as you will get chilled after spending an hour at a time underwater.

Isla de la Juventud

Also known in the past as the Isle of Parrots, Isle of Pirates and the Isle of Pines, the **Isla de la Juventud** (Isle of Youth) is 80 km (50 miles) southwest of Cuba. A protected national park, the El Colony diving zone between Punta Frances and Punta Pedernales is superb, as much of the more fragile coral ecosystems are protected, resulting in a huge biodiversity to be found in over 50 dive sites. There are vertical walls with gorgonian sea fans, huge barrel sponges and tropical fish everywhere; you will find steep coral slopes, caves, caverns and tunnels, individual coral 'bommies' and submarine peaks that just defy description.

Not to be outdone, the fish populations also change with large aggregations of snapper and grunt on some reefs, big Nassau Grouper (*Epinephelus striatus*) on others, barracuda, sharks, turtles and other pelagics on more exposed sites. Eagle rays are common, as are Creole Wrasse (*Clepticus parrae*), Blue Chromis (*Chromis cyanea*) and Fairy Basslets (*Gramma loreto*), their purple and orange bodies very obvious under the coral overhangs. Dive sites such as **Pared de Coral Negro**, **Tunel del Amor**, **Cueva Azul**, **El Pasaje Escondido**, **Cueva de los Sabalos**, **Piedra de Coral**, **El Salto**, **Paraiso de las Levisas** and **Pequeno Reino** are all individually superb, but these are just a small portion of what is available along the south coast keys. Also often called the Island of a Thousand Names, there are over 600 small coral islands, cayes and sandbars, many of which have a nice sheltered lagoon on the inside and a sheer vertical wall on the ocean side. The Canarreos Archipelago in particular is simply stunning and has still not been fully explored.

Previous page: Clockwise from top left: old American cars are a symbol of Cuba; small dive boats take only a handful of divers at any one time out to the reefs of the Gardens of the Queen; you can even encounter saltwater crocodiles or Caiman amongst the mangroves; schools of Horse-eye Jacks (Caranx latus) are commonly found on most reefs.

Opposite: Huge sea fans tipped with crinoids can be found along the edge of the vertical walls, as they prefer shallow well-aerated water and sunlight.

Below: Hawksbill Turtles (Eretmochelys imbricata) are the most commonly seen turtle here as many lay their eggs on the beaches.

Los Jardines de la Reina

Around 100 km (62 miles) southwest of central mainland Cuba are some 250 small coral islands set in a crystal-clear water shallow on one side and with great depth on the other. Known collectively as the **Los Jardines de la Reina** (Gardens of the Queen), the dive sites are as interesting as they are diverse, with virtually every coral habitat that you can find in the Caribbean. Stretched over 120 km (75 miles) and at times over 32 km (20 miles) wide, the marine park is unpopulated. There are the classic 'spur and groove' formations, vertical walls, tunnels, peaks, caverns, mangrove forests, garden eel beds, anemone gardens and, of course, sharks.

Juraco on the mainland is your embarkation point onto one of only a small handful of live-aboards that explore these waters, which are now the largest protected marine area in the Caribbean. There are shark-feeding experiences similar to those in the Bahamas, but here there are also huge grouper, which are also fed. Excursions into the mangrove lagoons will reveal huge schools of silverside minnows, tons of small invertebrates and even saltwater crocodiles!

Above: Los Jardines de la Reina have some of the least dived reefs in the Caribbean. Now a marine national park, there are only a handful of dive boats which visit these waters.

Maria la Gorda

At the extreme western tip of Cuba in the Ensenada de Corrientes protected diving zone is **Maria la Gorda**. The bay opposite the resort can be explored easily by snorkelling as there are many small isolated coral heads. A couple of large piers are built out onto this sandy platform and a handful of small dive boats will take you out to the huge variety of dive sites found nearby.

Many of the shallower coral heads are protected by a huge buttress reef that is formed along the edge of the wall with wide sandy slopes that drop down into the depths. Gorgonian sea fans, barrel sponges, elkhorn and staghorn corals are plentiful and you will usually come across large schools of Horse-eye Jacks (*Caranx latus*) and fusiliers. The region is not that well known for its quality of corals and marine life, compared to other regions, but what is here is still plentiful, varied and interesting.

There are over 50 dive sites and diver numbers on the boats are limited. All the dive sites are fairly close, so you only do one dive at a time, then return for the next dive group to go out; this is repeated in the afternoon. **Paraiso Perdido** (Paradise Lost) has depths from 18–30 m (60–100 ft) and has a high intensity of sponges and small sea fans, with lots of holes for small critters to hide in. **Ancla del Pirata** (Pirate's Anchor) is in 15 m (50 ft) on a coral garden around two large anchors resting up against the coral mini-wall. **Las Tetas de Maria** (Maria's Breasts) are two large rounded coral bommies with a sandy lane between them. Usually filled with small tropical fish, the maximum depth here is 24 m (80 ft).

Above: Ancient ships' anchors lie dotted all over the reef, completely encrusted in coral growth, their history or origin unknown.

Cayman Islands

The Cayman Islands consist of three inhabited islands: Grand Cayman, Little Cayman and Cayman Brac, and Owen Island, which is a small bird sanctuary. Grand Cayman is the largest of the islands at 35 km (22 miles) long and is famous for a small area of the North Sound where tourists and divers can have the experience of a lifetime, swimming and feeding a group of wild stingrays. Just recently a new shipwreck has been added to their repertoire of diving sites, the *Kittiwake* lies off Seven Mile Beach in shallow water.

Little Cayman lies 120 km (75 miles) northeast of Grand Cayman, and is the third and smallest of the group. It is only 14.5 km long (9 miles) by 1.6 km (1 mile) at its widest point. Owen Island is located along the south shore of Little Cayman. You can snorkel out to the island which is about 200 m (660 ft) offshore.

Across the channel from Little Cayman lies Cayman Brac, which is 20 km (12 miles) long by just over 1.6 km (1 mile) wide.

There are over 1,000 recorded dive sites around all three of the Cayman Islands with many more sites found each year to replace overdived sites and allow the reef time to replenish and recover from any possible diver trauma. However, world-famous dives such as the sandbar and Stingray City are on whenever the conditions are perfect, as the site is a low impact area. While Grand Cayman is the obvious Mecca for most sport divers, I place the Sister Islands of Little Cayman and Cayman Brac at the top of my diving ladder. Much smaller and more intimate, the Sister Islands are perfect for 'get away from it all' type of diving with absolutely superb vertical walls, excellent wrecks and a wealth of marine life that is almost unparallelled in the Caribbean.

Opposite: Clockwise from top left: the 'Bluff' or cliff off the east end of Cayman Brac rises over 40 m (140 ft); Little Cayman Island is home to the legendary Bloody Bay Marine Park; tiny Christmas Tree Worms (Spirobranchus giganteus) are both light- and pressure-sensitive; Stingray City and the Sandbar in the North Sound of Grand Cayman are still regarded as the best sites for stingray encounters in the Caribbean.

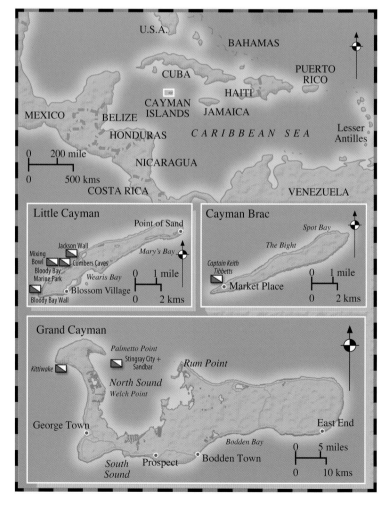

TRAVEL ADVISORY CAYMAN ISLANDS

Climate: Air temperatures average between 30–40° C (86–104° F) in the summer. Hurricane season is June to November, so expect squalls. January and February are considered the winter months and evening temperatures can be cool.

When to go: May to September is best for great visibility; however, you can dive all year round as there is always a lee shore and great reef or wreck nearby for you to explore.

Getting there: The Caymans are serviced by many international airline carriers from the USA, UK and Canada. Their own airline, Cayman Airways, also operates from many destinations including Honduras, Cuba, Jamaica and the USA. It is with Cayman Airways that you will connect to both Little Cayman and Cayman Brac. The Cayman Islands Aggressor yacht, a diver live-aboard, operates between all three islands.

Water temperature: From around 22° C (72° F) in December to 29° C (84° F) in July. Visibility is usually around 25–30 m (80–100 ft).

Quality of marine life: Very good, but some of the reefs off Seven Mile Beach are in rather a poor state, although the fish life is still prolific. Grand Cayman's North Wall, Little Cayman's Bloody Bay Wall and the north shore of Cayman Brac are all excellent with great features and tons of marine life.

Depth of dives: First dives are always to 30 m (100 ft) followed by a shallower dive to 12–18 m (40–60 ft). There are deeper dives, of course, and the Cayman Islands have superb technical diving services at Divetech.

Dive practicalities: Small boat trips are always exposed and windy, so extra sunscreen is a necessity; travel-calm tablets are also important, as there may be periods when you are sitting around in a rocking boat waiting for time to pass before the next dive.

Grand Cayman

Grand Cayman is home to one of the most legendary animal encounters on the planet. Dubbed the world's 'greatest 12-ft dive', the region lies inside the northern barrier reef which protects North Sound from the vagaries of wind and rough seas. Here the waters are almost always calm and sheltered and the curious behaviour of the stingrays was first recorded by local fishermen many years ago. The fishermen used to clean their fish catches at the end of each day in the shallows near the edge of the drop-off and noticed that many stingrays would come in to take advantage of this free meal. Once the cleaning was over, the rays soon got bored and went about their normal business foraging the sand flats for small crabs, snails and burrowing sea urchins.

The stingray most commonly found in the Cayman Islands is the Southern Stingray (*Dasyatis americana*) and the two locations where they principally congregate in the North Sound are **Stingray City** which is around 3–5 m (10–17 ft) deep and the **Sandbar**, a natural sandy plateau around only 1 m (3 ft 3 in) deep.

Below: Stingray City and the much shallower Sandbar offer divers and snorkellers the unique and safe opportunity to swim and interact with large numbers of the Southern Stingrays (Dasyatis americana).

The deeper dive site has fewer visitors, but the shallow sandbar region is still inundated by large numbers of tourist boats. Once in position, the boat staff will introduce some food into the water to attract the rays. The surge of excitement is palpable as the rays swoop in and envelop you in their 'wings' in the search of a free meal. If you do get the chance to feed them, hold the squid in the palm of your hand. The sensation is similar to feeding a horse – underwater. It is advisable to wear some sort of body protection, such as a thin wetsuit or skin, as the stingrays have been known to give a rather nasty suction bite.

The *Kittiwake*

The *Kittiwake* was a former United States Submarine Rescue Vessel scuttled off Seven Mile Beach in January 2011. Situated on a wide sandy plain, before you reach the buttress reef and the outer wall, the *Kittiwake* lies parallel to the shore. The shallowest parts are only 1 m (3 ft 3 in) deep and the deepest around 25 m (80 ft) making her perfect for divers and snorkellers of all levels.

Below: The Kittiwake, a former US Naval Rescue vessel, was sunk as a diver attraction on 5 January 2011. Now well overgrown with algae and small corals, it is already home to a huge diversity of fish and invertebrates.

Little Cayman

Bloody Bay Marine Park along the north shore of **Little Cayman** is one of the most spectacular and varied dive locations in the world. Of the 56 listed dive sites around this island, 18 lie along **Bloody Bay** and **Jackson Walls**. Bloody Bay was made a marine park in 1987 and hosts two separate walls. To the east is Jackson Wall, while Bloody Bay Wall lies to the west, but both are known as Bloody Bay Marine Park.

Virtually all of the dives are potentially deep ones, with the reef plummeting over 1,800 m (6,000 ft), but as the wall starts at only 6 m (20 ft), you can plan a variable profile dive and spend as much time as you want in the shallows.

Mixing Bowl at the juncture of both Bloody Bay and Jackson Bight has that superb combination of a shallow start to a near vertical and undercut wall, as well as a more gently sloping wall cut with large fissures. The area is home to several large Nassau Grouper (*Epinephelus striatus*) which almost agitate you to take their photographs.

Visibility is always great on the vertical part of the wall as any detritus quickly drops into the depths. The underhanging ledges have large black coral trees tipped with strawberry sponges, Hawksbill Turtles (*Eretmochelys imbricata*) are always found along the reef edge and plenty of tropical reef fish are found including cowfish, angelfish, Yellow Snapper (*Ocyurus chrysurus*) and triggerfish.

Further along to the east is **Cumbers Caves** which is potentially a deep dive. With little or no current on the inner reef and visibility over 60 m (200 ft), the caves are actually a series of sand chutes which cut through the coral aeons ago and the coral has grown back over the ravines. To start this dive on the inner reef sandy plain and descend out onto the wall is breathtaking. I experienced a real feeling of vertigo on this dive. This is a point to be remembered on all potentially bottomless wall dives.

The area is also well known for its large numbers of anemones and their attendant Diamond-backed Blennies (*Malacoctenus boehlkei*) and Yellow-headed Jawfish (*Opistognathus aurifrons*). A garden eel colony is found in the sand flats and large numbers of lionfish.

Opposite: Bloody Bay Wall is regarded as one of the top dives of the Caribbean. With vertical walls that start in only 6 m (20 ft), crystal-clear water and superb marine life encounters, no wonder it has become a Mecca for divers.

Above: Overfriendly Nassau Grouper (Epinephelus striatus) are common on a number of dive sites along Bloody Bay Wall. They are so used to divers that they actually become a nuisance when you are trying to take photographs.

Cayman Brac

Most dives are undertaken along the north shore of Cayman Brac. Virtually all of the wreck sites are here, as well as some absolutely cracking reef dives. Undoubtedly the top dive is the re-christened MV **Captain Keith Tibbetts**, a former Russian frigate. The ship is 95 m long (330 ft) with a beam of 12.8 m (42.6 ft). Originally part of the old Soviet fleet stationed in Cuba during the Cold War, the vessel was never actually involved in any conflict. She was bought by the Cayman Islands government to be sunk as a diver attraction and finally dropped to her new home in September 1996.

Large pelagics usually swim by with barracuda and Horse-eye Jacks a common sight. Known simply as the **356**, the wreck is quite clearly the premier dive on all three islands.

Other small wrecks nearby are the *Kissimme, Topsy, Cayman Mariner* and the *Barbara Ann*, all in depths of around 12–25 m (40–80 ft) and well covered with marine life. All of the wrecks are adjacent to good coral reefs and are usually used as night dives when the reef comes alive with small squid, lobster, red night shrimps and octopus.

Opposite above: Peacock Flounders (Bothus lunatus) are a common sand-dwelling fish. Usually shy, they can be approached with patience.

Opposite below: A lifelong mating pair of Grey Angelfish (Pomacanthus arcuatus) are regularly found on the spur and groove reefs of the Cayman Islands.

Below: Completely covered with all manner of sponges, soft corals and small sea fans, the Captain Keith Tibbetts is home to reef fish, tiny invertebrates and a few resident turtles.

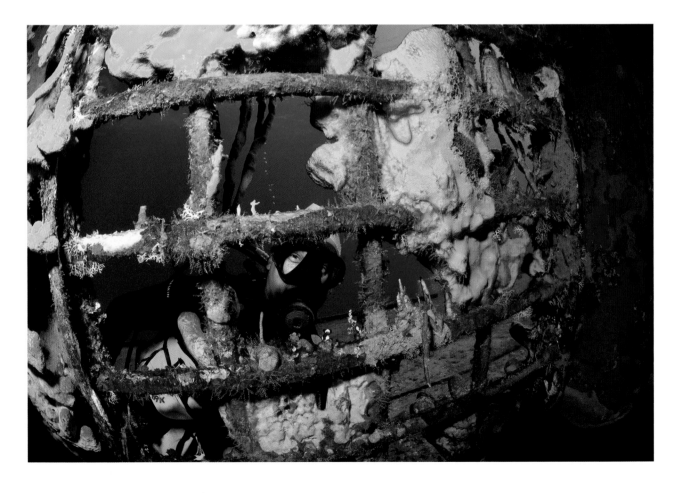

West Caribbean

Offshore from Belize are over 450 islands and coral cayes amid the second-longest coral barrier reef in the world. The coastline is predominantly marshland and mosquito heaven, but once you venture out to the islands and atolls where the diving is concentrated, you are well clear of this. The diving off the coral atolls is regarded by many as world class.

The Bay Islands of Honduras comprise Roatán, Guanaja and Utila and are found 64 km (40 miles) to the north of the mainland. This is where all of the scuba diving is concentrated. Roatán is the largest at around 58 km (36 miles) long. It is much easier to do the diving here by live-aboard boat, as this will give you the widest variety of dives for the least amount of effort. Guanaja to the northeast is dominated by its three large peaks and surrounded by a barrier reef. These closely packed reefs offer superb protection for the coral growth. Sponges are prevalent and all of the associated tropical marine life of the Caribbean appears to have made its home here. Utila has become known for its sightings of Whale Sharks (*Rhincodon typus*).

Opposite: Horse-eye Jacks (Caranx latus) school in large numbers over reefs and wrecks.

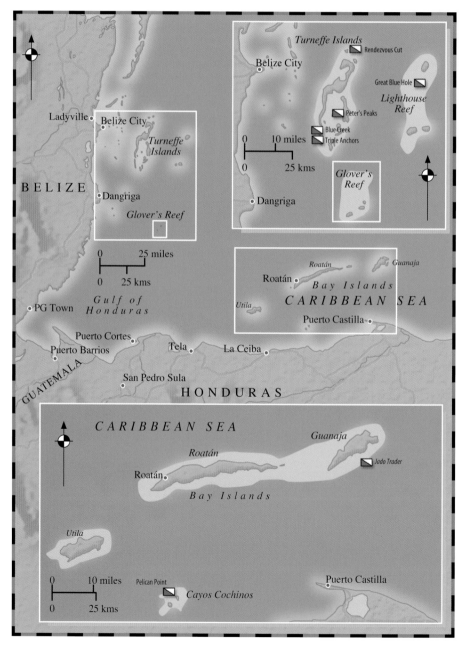

TRAVEL ADVISORY BELIZE

Climate: Tropical, usually combined with high humidity. Average temperatures in the coastal regions range from 24° C (75° F) in January to 27° C (81° F) in July. Temperatures are slightly higher inland, except for the southern highland plateaus where it is noticeably cooler year round. Overall, the seasons are marked more by differences in humidity and rainfall than in temperature, except offshore when the cooler sea breezes are always more noticeable.

When to go: Diving is available all year round, but squalls from both the Pacific and eastern Caribbean can pound some of the outer reefs. Hurricanes rarely come until October and November, but be prepared for some heavy rainfall in those periods.

Getting there: Belize City is your embarkation point. It is not exactly the place that you would want to hang around in, but transfers are quick and easy by boat to the outer reef resorts or by picking up your live-aboard to get the best of all three atolls.

Water temperature: Sea temperatures vary from around 22° C (72° F) in December to 29° C (84° F) in July. Visibility is usually around 25–30 m (80–100 ft).

Quality of marine life: There are some huge schools of fish to be found on the outer reefs; time around the mangroves is always interesting for little critters, but it is the sheer spectacle of the area that always impresses.

Depth of dives: Averages around 25 m (80 ft) but you will be pushing the boundaries of safe diving limits in the Great Blue Hole to get among the stalactites.

Dive practicalities: Small boat trips are always exposed and windy, so extra sunscreen is a necessity, travel-calm tablets are also important, as there may be periods when you are sitting around in a rocking boat waiting for time to pass before the next dive.

TRAVEL ADVISORY HONDURAS BAY ISLANDS

Climate: Hot and humid almost all year round. Air temperatures rarely rise above 32° C (90° F) in the summer. Hurricane season is June to November, so expect squalls coming in overland from the Pacific. Otherwise there are nice even easterly breezes from the Caribbean. The Caribbean coast can experience a lot of rain, the heaviest being from September to February.

When to go: May to September is best for great visibility; however, you can dive all year round as there is always a lee shore and great reef or wreck nearby for you to explore. February and March are Whale Shark season off Utila.

Getting there: San Pedro Sula on mainland Honduras is the central hub for connections from the United States. Air Islena flies direct to all three Bay Islands, but these small aircraft have notorious weight restrictions. Boats and ferries can be boarded at La Ceiba for connections to Roatán and Utila.

Water temperature: Average 26° C (80° F) all year round. Visibility is usually around 25–30 m (80–100 ft).

Quality of marine life: Above average collection of the best of what is on offer in the Caribbean, including Manta Rays off Cayos Cochinos and Whale Sharks off Utila. Much of the best of the diving is to be found in less than 12 m (40 ft) and night dives to these depths always have a high yield of interesting critters.

Depth of dives: First dives are always to 30 m (100 ft) followed by a shallower dive to 12–18 m (40–60 ft).

Dive practicalities: There are a number of very professional dive shops, but the dive sites available are fairly restricted, so it is often better to opt for the Aggressor live-aboard dive boat to cruise the entire area. The Bay Islands are also notorious for some of the most aggressive no-see-ums anywhere. Bring lots of repellent.

Belize: Turneffe Atoll

The 200 islands and cayes of **Turneffe Reef** form the largest of the three atolls in Belize. The atoll is around 56 km (35 miles) long and over 16 km (10 miles) at its widest point.

Most of the eastern shoreline is protected by a continuous barrier reef over 56 km (35 miles) long. The reef structure on this typical Caribbean exposed reef is of spur and groove formation with 'fingers' of coral growth separated by sandy valleys. The western edge of the atoll is quite shallow with plenty of sand and few good corals. The northeastern parts are constantly buffeted by big long Caribbean swells making diving conditions virtually non-existent. Much of the diving is located around the more sheltered southwestern area of the atoll. When the sea conditions are perfect, the east coast offers up huge concentrations of fish with Horse-eye Jacks (*Caranx latus*), Dogtooth Snapper (*Lutjanus jocu*), fusiliers, Black Snapper (*Lutjanus cyanopterus*), grunt and Permit (*Trachinotus falcatus*). Invariably such large concentrations of fish also attract the larger predators such as Caribbean Reef Sharks (*Carcharhinus perezii*), but you also will see large tuna, barracuda, Wahoo (*Acanthocybium solandri*), King Mackerel (*Scomberomorus cavalla*) and even dolphins.

Blue Creek is named for the tidal pass that separates the outer reef from a mangrove lagoon. It has a maximum depth of only 11 m (35 ft) and is used regularly by the live-aboard dive boats as there is safe anchorage and an easy night dive within the channel. **Peter's Peaks** is down a sloping sandy plane to reach the buttress reef inner mini-wall which rises 5 m (17 ft) above you. To get to the outer wall, you either ascend to drop over or find one of the many tunnels that cut under the reef bringing you out on the wall at 25 m (80 ft). **Triple Anchors** is south past Blue Creek and has the typical formations of scattered coral heads on a sandy slope before the spur and groove reef starts. The average depth is 12–16 m (40–60 ft) where you may see the scattered remains of an 18th-century sailing vessel with three anchors very visible, even though they are well encrusted.

Above: A close up of Symmetrical Brain Coral (Diploria strigosa), growing over 2 m (6 ft 6 in) in size, these corals are very common throughout the Caribbean region and play host to various cleaning gobies.

Rendezvous Cut is usually one of the first dives that you will do in the area, coming out of San Pedro, with an average depth of only 12–15 m (40–50 ft). There are good stands of Elkhorn Coral (*Acropora palmata*), large brain and boulder corals.

Left: Most small caverns and undercut ledges have small schools of various species of snapper and grunt. Fairly easy to approach, they are unafraid of divers.

Below: Large Great Barracuda (Sphyraena barracuda) are solitary fish around these islands, rarely shoaling unlike their counterparts in the Indo-Pacific.

Lighthouse Reef

Over 100 km (60 miles) east into the Caribbean, **Lighthouse Reef** is the furthest offshore from Belize City; however, it is still visited by day boats from San Pedro and by the various live-aboard vessels that work in the region. The interior of the lagoon is only around 2.7 m (9 ft) in depth. There are six coral cayes, with Sandbore Caye to the north which houses one of the two lighthouses on the atoll. Northern Caye has a new dive resort with mature mangroves and even a few saltwater crocodiles! Midway down the atoll is the **Great Blue Hole**, at over 90 m (300 ft) across and 145 m (480 ft) deep, there is little or no coral within its rim, just some small stubby specimens of hard coral and Venus Sea Fans (*Gorgonia flabellum*). The depth of the shaft allows little light to penetrate. This restricts coral growth, and so there are also very few fish. At about 40 m (130 ft) a large cut appears and it is here that you see the first of the huge stalactites that stretch down from the 'ceiling'. Many extend more than 6 m (20 ft) down into the abyss, where the first of the Bull Sharks (*Carcharhinus leucas*) may be seen. As you leave the confines of the cavern, you may see sharks at close quarters in a seemingly bottomless pit! It is only when you start to ascend that you are aware of some of the smaller critters that live in the upper reaches of the shaft, such as Pederson Cleaner Shrimps (*Periclimenes pedersoni*), Corkscrew Anemones (*Macrodactyla doreensis*) and many juvenile reef fish which have found a safe haven away from the open reef.

Above: Most of the walls are cut by massive fissures which lead into the inner reefs. Buoyancy control and attention to your depth limits are very important here.

Opposite: Caribbean Reef Octopus (Octopus briareus) are a delight to find on any reef at night. If disturbed when hunting, these octopuses turn the most amazing aquamarine blue colour, as they cast their 'fleshy' net over their prey.

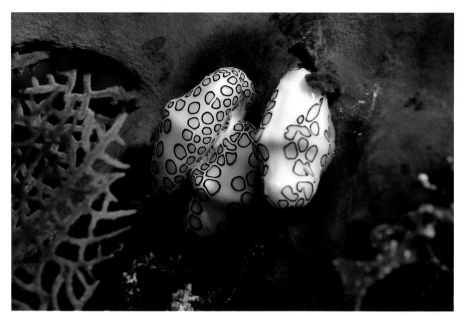

Left: The shallows have Flamingo Tongue shells (pictured), large Channel Clinging Crabs (Mithrax spinosissimus), Sailfin Blennies (Emblemaria pandionis), octopus, Golden Stingrays (Urolophus jamaicensis) and Orange-ball Anemones (Pseudocorynactis caribbeorum).

Opposite: Schools of Tarpon (Megalops atlanticus) hang out in the shallow caverns waiting for night to fall before they start to hunt in the shallow reefs.

Honduras: Hog Islands

Diving around the **Bay Islands** is varied and as usual the further you are offshore, the better the quality of corals and marine life. There are mini-walls, steep vertical walls undercut with caves and caverns, sand chutes, tunnels and sandy planes that are all just filled with marine life. South of Roatán is Cayos Cochinos or **Hog Islands**. These are a series of two larger islands and around ten small coral cayes. **Pelican Point**'s reef crest is only 3 m (10 ft) below the surface and then it plummets down a vertical wall into the depths. There are numerous caves and caverns, tunnels and underhanging walls. The coral life here is exceptional. The reef crest and lip are perfect for night diving as you can easily have over an hour underwater with no time penalty.

Guanaja: The *Jado Trader*

The former refrigerated transport ship **Jado Trader** was scuttled in 1987 as a dive site attraction southwest of Southwest Cay of Guanaja. The ship is 73 m (240 ft) long and lies on her starboard side in depths ranging from 25–33 m (80–110 ft), lodged near two huge coral pinnacles that rise to within 9 m (30 ft) of the surface. Completely open in aspect, the top areas of the superstructure, masts and rigging are covered in long rope sponges, deepwater gorgonian sea fans and crinoids. Every part of her interior is covered in *Tubastrea* Golden Cup Corals and her winch mechanism is a palette of red, green and yellow encrusting sponges. While this is a deep dive, the ship is a superb addition to an otherwise fairly drab reef.

Netherlands Antilles

Also known as the Dutch Antilles, the Netherlands Antilles comprise two island groups of three islands each. The Leeward Islands group includes Saba, Sint Eustatius and Sint Maarten which is the southern half of St Martin that is shared with France. Aruba, Bonaire and Curaçao, collectively known as the ABCs, are described as being in the Windward Islands and are covered here.

Discovered in 1499, they were originally settled by the Spanish, then taken over by the Dutch East India Company in the 17th century. The islands have remained under Dutch jurisdiction. The principal industry is the processing of oil from the Venezuela oil fields, but scuba diving tourism is a massive market – not only for nearby American tourists, but also for native Dutch. Cruise ships are another large sector of the market. While Dutch is the official language throughout all six islands, English is widely spoken (certainly in the dive centres because most are owned and operated by Americans).

The ABCs are undoubtedly very high on most divers' wish list and many make the pilgrimage annually to savour the hundreds of dive sites that are found around these quaint islands that combine a curious mixture of arid, cactus-filled landscape, wonderful salt pans, flamingos, colourful Caribbean/Dutch architecture, awful oil refineries and some of the best reefs and marine life to be found in the Caribbean.

Opposite: Clockwise from top left: juvenile Trumpetfish (Aulostomus maculatus) hide amidst the branches of finger corals as they are virtually the same shape; the rugged shores and clear waters of Bonaire are very popular with divers for shore diving; Lettuce Leaf Seaslugs (Tridachia crispata) feed principally on the algae which grow over dead coral; large schools of Bigeye Scad (Selar crumenophthalmus) are a common sight in many locations.

TRAVEL ADVISORY NETHERLANDS ANTILLES

Climate: Considered to be outside the hurricane belt, therefore enjoying a much more stable climate. Easterly trade winds keep humidity low and air temperatures rarely rise above 32° C (90° F) in the summer. There is little rain and it usually falls from October to December resulting in a very arid aspect.

When to go: May to September is best for great visibility; however, you can dive all year round as there is always a lee shore and great reef or wreck nearby for you to explore.

Getting there: Direct flights via Trinidad and Miami are available to all three islands, which in turn are serviced by all of the major airlines. KLM flies direct from Amsterdam.

Water temperature: Average 27° C (80° F) all year round. Visibility is usually around 25–30 m (80–100 ft).

Quality of marine life: Known for seahorses, frogfish and a few other rarer critters. On top of that, great reefs and an abundance of fish make the dives very good indeed.

Depth of dives: First dives are always to 30 m (100 ft) followed by a shallower dive to 12–18m (40–60 ft).

Dive practicalities: Good buoyancy is essential, particularly in the shipwrecks. Much of the diving can be done from the shore so avoiding the extra expense of boat dives. Full suits are recommended against fire coral and stinging hydroids which you may touch accidentally.

Aruba: Pos Chiquito/Snapper City

Southeast of Pos Chiquito is a dive site that is sometimes called **Snapper City** principally because of the number and variety of snapper which are found on the reef. Diveable from the shore, Pos Chiquito has large star, boulder and brain corals dotted with various sea fans and large soft corals. Looking closely between the strands of polyps, you will find delicate pufferfish and filefish and juvenile cornetfish. This site is very similar to a number nearby including **Mangel Halto Reef** and **Isla de Oro Reef**, all of which have a quite steep slope down to around 34 m (110 ft). There are great sea fans, deepwater gorgonians, sheet and lace coral that stretch out into the current amid tube sponges and barrel sponges. Staghorn (*Acropora cervicornis*) and Elkhorn Corals (*Acropora palmata*) are found in the shallows and the older reef, deeper down, has many small undercut ledges where nurse sharks, moray eels and lobster can be found. A current should be expected on this dive and it brings with it nutrient-rich waters which help feed the Manta Rays (*Manta birostris*) that also frequent this area of the coast (if you are lucky!).

The *Antilla*

Often referred to as the Ghost Ship, this 122 m (400 ft) German freighter was scuttled in shallow water near Aruba's northwest point in 1940. The *Antilla* was in the Caribbean collecting fuel from the nearby refinery to supply to German U-boats. When Germany invaded Holland in 1940, the Dutch authorities sought to impound this German vessel. Rather than surrender to the 'enemy', the captain scuttled the ship where she lay at anchor.

Parts of her superstructure are still high and dry and act as roosts for pelicans and terns. The bows are only in 9 m (30 ft) and her stern in 18 m (60 ft) making her one of the best wreck-diving sites in the entire Caribbean. The upper starboard side of the ship resembles a coral wall and is home to everything that you would expect to find on a good healthy reef. The superstructure is quite open now and easily negotiable, but care should be taken that your dive equipment does not get snagged. Due to its shallow depth, the site is often done at night.

Opposite above: Elkhorn Coral (Acropora palmat) has stout branches which face into the ocean swell. Preferring shallow, well-lit and aerated water, this coral has been the demise of many shipwrecks in the past.

Above: Known as 'Mas Bongo', massive schools of juvenile trevally congregate under piers, swirling around the supports to evade larger predators.

Opposite below Juvenile Queen Angelfish (Holacanthus ciliaris) have the most outrageous colours when they are young, the adults are equally as vivid.

Bonaire: Town Pier

The **Town Pier** is probably the most popular dive site in Bonaire, so it does get very busy. You could just detach from the main group and treat the dive very much like a 'muck dive' in Indonesia. There are lots of interesting little spider crabs, arrow crabs, pipefish, sharptailed eels, moray eels, large numbers of cornetfish, frogfish and seahorses. At only 11 m (37 ft) deep, time and depth are not an issue.

Below The Longsnout Seahorse (Hippocampus reidi) *is relatively rare around many Caribbean islands but some locations are well known for them and you are almost guaranteed to spot one.*

The *Hilma Hooker*

The 74 m (242 ft) *Hilma Hooker* was originally built in the Netherlands in 1951 and had to make port in Kralendijk due to problems with her rudder in 1984. Moored at the Town Pier, port authorities became suspicious of her, and on further inspection of the ship discovered a false bulkhead that hid 11,340 kg (25,000 lb) of marijuana. The crew was subsequently arrested and the ship impounded. No trace of her owners could be found, but her rapidly deteriorating condition was causing concern, so she was towed to the southern end of the island where she sank five days later on 7 September 1984.

Now lying on her starboard side in around 30 m (100 ft) of water she is quite open in aspect. Her wheelhouse is open and navigable, but due to her depth and time constraints, divers are recommended to have some wreck-diving experience. Located at the beginning of the double reefs that are synonymous with this region of Bonaire, there is good coral and algae growth on her as well as rope sponges, small hard corals and sea fans. Nearby are two very good reef dives, **Angel City** and **Alice in Wonderland** where barracuda, large tarpon and numerous angelfish are a speciality.

Above *Night diving on reefs and wrecks is always excellent due to the amount of invertebrate life which comes out after dusk. This Red Night Shrimp (Rhynchocinetes rigens) is very common and easily spotted by its reflective green eyes.*

Curaçao: Mushroom Forest

Mushroom Forest near the westerly point of Curaçao is around 20 minutes from the nearest dive centre and is very distinctive. In 13 m (43 ft) of water Pillar Coral (*Dendrogyra cylindrus*) has curiously covered an area of reef top in tall finger-shaped formations with a bulbous 'mushroom-like' head. There are always parrotfish, wrasse, small eels, schooling Blue Tangs (*Acanthurus coeruleus*) and plenty of butterflyfish and angelfish. Nearby is a large cavern cut into the coral platform, the sides of which are smothered in Golden Cup Corals, so remember to bring your dive light to penetrate the murky depths. Schools of silverside minnows and hatchetfish are found here.

Swimming out towards the shelf and the edge of the wall, there are large numbers of giant anemones with cleaner shrimps on them. Stay still long enough and you will see large grouper and jacks coming close into the shelf to be cleaned of parasites. There are other small caverns at **Playa Lagun** to the north of Mushroom Forest. To the south of Mushroom Forest is **Sponge Forest**, home to huge organpipe sponges, rich in chromis and Sergeant Majors (*Abudefduf saxatilis*).

Opposite The former Tugboat wreck on Curaçao is a nice easy dive situated part way between the steeply sloping outer wall and the mini-wall adjacent to the shore.

The *Superior Producer*

The *Superior Producer* is just one of a number of superb dive sites stretching along the south shore of Curaçao. The overloaded freighter was on her way to Venezuela back in 1977 when she caught the wrong wave at the entrance to the port and quickly sank.

Resting upright in 32 m (105 ft) of water, the ship is relatively intact. Her holds are open and the beams above are also covered in sponges and corals, so care should be taken when exiting the wreck. Good buoyancy control is essential on the dive. Believe it or not, a special charter helicopter will take divers out to the site, giving you great aerial views of the city, then dropping you off in open water over the wreck! The site is also done as a shore dive, but arriving by boat is obviously the more comfortable option. Time is limited due to her depth and you will want to come back again for a night dive.

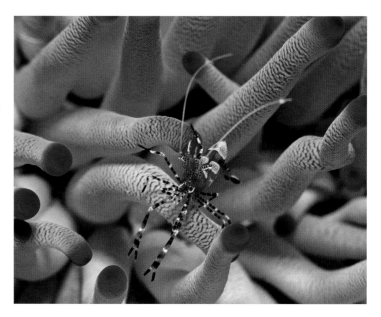

Above Bubble-tip Anemones (Entacmaea quadricolor) quite often have commensal shrimps living amidst their tentacles. Acting as cleaner shrimps, they hop off and service passing fish.

Tobago

Trinidad and Tobago lie on the continental shelf of South America, and are therefore geologically and geographically considered to lie entirely in South America. However, because of their proximity to the Caribbean and other Leeward Islands and their English language heritage, they are classed as being in North America.

A Spanish colony after the arrival of Columbus in 1498 until the takeover by the British in 1797, the island of Tobago changed hands several times and was finally ceded to Britain in 1802. The country gained full independence in 1962 and became a republic in 1976. Trinidad's economy is largely based around petrochemicals but Tobago relies strongly on tourism, particularly through the diving industry, though I should also mention cricket and carnivals here!

Known as the originators of the steel band, calypso and soca music, the 'vibe' of the islands is palpable, the locals are an amazing ethnic mix of Asian, Indian, African and British, all living in what would appear great racial harmony. Consequently things are pretty laid back, except for the amazing currents which push through between the islands from the Atlantic and upwards from the Orinoco delta.

Tobago occupies an area of about 310 sq km (120 sq miles) and is 40 km (25 miles) long and 12 km (7.5 miles) wide at its greatest extent. Its interior boasts the oldest protected rainforest in the world, its underwater scenery is just as impressive and the seas are teeming with life, fed by the nutrient-rich waters of the Guyana Current. The island's exposure to the Atlantic, as well as its protected Caribbean shores, allow for that curious mix of both warm and colder water species, large numbers of pelagics including one of the world's permanent locations for Manta Rays (*Manta birostris*) and endemic species not found anywhere else.

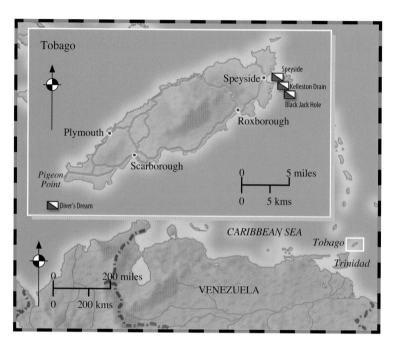

Opposite: Clockwise from top left: hidden amongst the sea fans, slender filefish are very small and sway in time with the current; the offshore reefs are shallower and swept by currents making for easy drift diving; known colloquially as 'Tobago taxis', Manta Rays (Manta birostris) are a regular feature of the diving at Speyside; our first experience of a tropical shallow reef is by snorkelling.

TRAVEL ADVISORY TOBAGO

Climate: Humidity is always high, despite those sea breezes, and even in December it can be as much as 94 per cent, but because of Tobago's southerly location, temperatures are pretty equable all year round. The rainy season is from June to November and the dry (carnival) season from December to May.

When to go: January to May when there is the least amount of rain, but the air temperatures will be cooler.

Getting there: International direct flights via Trinidad and most of the nearby islands with Liat and Winair. Larger commercial airlines all route through Trinidad.

Water temperature: Averages 27° C (80° F) all year round. Visibility is usually around 25–30 m (80–100 ft).

Quality of marine life: The Manta Rays of Speyside are breathtaking.

Depth of dives: Around 12–18 m (40–60 ft) as there is just so much life in shallower water; there are no really deep walls.

Dive practicalities: The current at the southern end of Tobago and around Speyside is constant. Speeds vary from between 1 knot to over 3 knots and divers must always be accompanied by a dive master with a surface marker buoy. All divers must be equipped with a whistle warning device and inflatable dayglo sausage in case of emergency.

Speyside

Speyside is a region within the bay to the west and south of Little Tobago Island and includes the reefs around Goat Island which is closer to shore. Speyside has some of the best diving in Tobago, particularly due to the chance of encountering giant Manta Rays, schools of tarpon and regular sightings of sharks. Most dives are drift dives and many areas are subject to oceanic surge. However, the majestic spectacle of the gigantic brain corals, the largest recorded in the northern hemisphere, and the zillions of tiny fish get divers and photographers coming back year after year.

Black Jack Hole is located on the southeastern shore of Little Tobago Island and is regarded as the easier precursor dive to Kelleston Drain. Easier because the current is not running quite so fast in this area and the dive terminates where the **Kelleston Drain** dive takes off.

Named after the frequently seen schools of Black Jacks (*Caranx lugubris*) the dive is probably better known for the massive shoals of Creole Wrasse (*Clepticus parrae*), and Blue Chromis (*Chromis cyanea*). As you venture further out from the shore, the current picks up and starts to whisk round towards Kelleston Drain. Using the coral plateau located off the southeastern corner as the starting point of the dive, the current carries you over the plateau into deeper water where the coral and sponge growth are much more profuse. This current not only enriches the sponges and smaller corals, it is also the main cause for what are regarded as the largest brain corals in the northern hemisphere. The Boulder Brain Corals (*Colpophyllia natans*) are so massive at over 6 m (20 ft) across that it is difficult to take in these ancient colonies of organisms as you sweep past in the current.

The Manta Rays located off Little Tobago Island are seen by divers on over 70 per cent of the dives. With a wingspan of over 6 m (20 ft), these graceful giants are now so used to observing divers in their domain that they are completely unperturbed by human presence and will remain in the divers' company for as much time as your air allows. This is truly a wonderful experience and Tobago is one of a handful of locations in the world (and the only site in the Caribbean) where you would expect to see large groups of Mantas all year round.

Opposite above: Speyside in Tobago has another claim to fame, other than Manta Rays (Manta birostris). It is home to the largest brain corals found in the entire Caribbean. Some of the large domes are easily over 4 m (13 ft) across and are fed by the constant tidal stream which comes through from South America.

Above: One of the more comical looking crustaceans is the Yellow-line Arrow Crab (Stenorhynchus seticornis). They are quite happy to forage day and night.

Opposite below: Goliath Grouper (Epinephelus itijara) patrol the shallow reefs and often hide inside the larger wrecks. They are often found with attached remora suckerfish which have become detached from their host Manta Rays.

Left: *Many species of blenny are found amongst the Caribbean reefs. Fulfilling a similar function to anemonefish or clownfish in the Pacific, Diamond Blennies (Malacoctenus boehlkei) live amongst the anemone's tentacles, immune from their stinging cells.*

Below: *Peppermint Gobies (Coryphopterus lipernes) and other cleaning gobies work around brain corals and other hard boulder corals, signalling to fish that the 'shop is open' to be cleaned of parasites.*

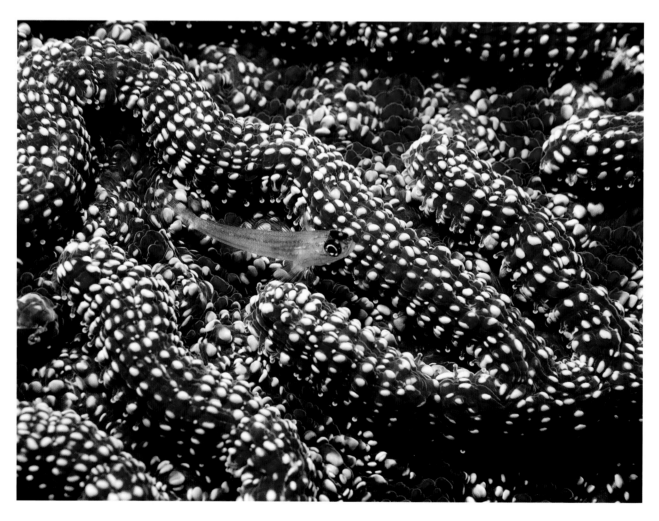

Diver's Dream

The dive boat motors out 8 km (5 miles) southwest of Pigeon Point to the shallow reefs around Drew Shoal to the drift dive at **Diver's Dream**. The shallowest part is only 6 m (20 ft) deep and the exposed limestone ridges slope gently down to around 15 m (50 ft). Divers have been known to be swept away and held under by the current, surfacing many hundreds of metres from the boat. This dive is exhilarating to say the least and not to be undertaken lightly.

The predominant feature of the dive is the thousands of Giant Barrel Sponges (*Xestospongia muta*), some are over 2 m (6 ft) across, but all are bent and misshapen by the current. The openings in the top of the sponges are squashed flat in many cases and all around them are dark Volcano Sponges (*Calyx podatypa*), orange Elephant Ear Sponges (*Agelas clathrodes*), large Deepwater Sea Fans (*Iciligorgia schrammi*) and Feather Brush Hydroids (*Dentitheca dendritica*). Nurse sharks rest in the sandy areas beneath the boulders and Queen Angelfish are seen all over the reef.

Below: The drift diving off the shallow offshore reefs is great fun, but not to be undertaken without due care and planning, as well as a very experienced boat skipper. Nurse sharks are always found on these dives.

Lesser Antilles

Including the British Virgin Islands, Dominica and St Lucia, these islands are all in the Eastern Caribbean. The Virgin Islands is the official name, but people often add 'British' to the title to distinguish them from the 'Virgin Islands of the United States' which were incorporated in 1917. The Virgin Islands comprise Tortola, Virgin Gorda, Jost Van Dyke and Anegada. Their geographical position means that a fascinating diversity of marine life is found around these islands. Anegada has the largest barrier reef in the eastern Caribbean and third largest in the world and is reputed to have more shipwrecks around her shores than any other island in the Caribbean.

Dominica is the youngest of the Caribbean islands, and is still being formed by geothermal activity. It contains the world's second-largest boiling lake and numerous hot springs, including some underwater. The topography is incredible with fantastic rainforest fauna and flora all found among cloud-topped peaks, dramatic gorges, caverns, waterfalls and hidden lakes. It is now recognized as a World Heritage Site. The underwater reefs also resemble more tropical dive sites because of the rarity of curious fish species, thousands of colourful crinoids, black coral forests and superb colorful sponges. Most of the diving is done on the sheltered western side of the island.

St Lucia is the second largest of the Windward Islands and is 43 km (27 miles) long and 23 km (14 miles) wide. Very mountainous and boasting the world's oldest protected rainforest, St Lucia is symbolized by the twin peaks of Soufrière called The Pitons, which dominate the landscape.

Opposite: Flying over the eastern Caribbean Islands is always a delight as it is only from the air that you can truly appreciate the scale and complexity of the land that can make island living so challenging.

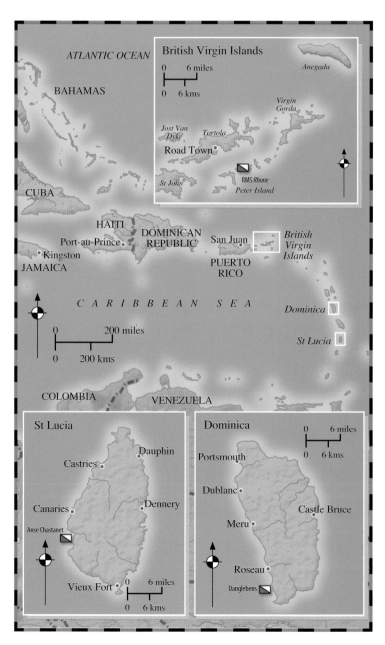

TRAVEL ADVISORY BRITISH VIRGIN ISLANDS

Climate: Subtropical, resulting in high humidity, but tempered by cool sea breezes. Generally very dry in the spring and summer months, temperatures can easily reach over 40° C (104° F). Increased rainfall during hurricane season from September to November.

When to go: Spring and autumn are usually superb with calm seas and light winds.

Getting there: Regular flights from all of the American hub airports, as well as flights from London, but all flights are first routed through San Juan in Puerto Rico.

Water temperature: Average 26° C (80° F), but can drop lower in the winter months. Visibility is usually around 25–30 m (80–100 ft).

Quality of marine life: Not known for brilliant corals – many of the rocks are covered only in low encrusting sponges, carpet corals and fire coral.

Depth of dives: Averages around 12–18 m (40–60 ft) but depths are greater on the *Rhone*, so care should be taken.

Dive practicalities: Care should be taken with exposure to the sun, particularly while travelling on the dive boats but take something warm to counteract the Arctic air-conditioning inside. Divers are advised to carry a torch particularly when exploring the *Rhone*.

TRAVEL ADVISORY ST LUCIA

Climate: Humidity is always high, with temperatures regularly hotter on the western (Caribbean) side of the island.

When to go: January to May are driest, but the air temperatures will be cooler. June to November is the rainy season.

Getting there: Direct flights are available to the island from the UK and American hubs, as well as short-haul flights from all of the neighbouring islands. Or there is a 300-seat catamaran ferry which operates between Guadeloupe, Dominica, Martinique and St Lucia.

Water temperature: Average 27° C (80° F) but can drop lower in the winter months. Visibility is usually around 25–30 m (80–100 ft).

Quality of marine life: Superb diversity of marine life and all mainly in shallow waters.

Depth of dives: Averages 12–18 m (40–60 ft). Deeper around the Pitons; the volcanic vents are at the edge of safe sport diving limits.

Dive practicalities: Water can be cooler in the south. A full suit is recommended against stings from marine life.

TRAVEL ADVISORY DOMINICA

Climate: Subtropical with rain recorded every month, totalling 216 cm (85 in) annually. Maximum and minimum temperatures never stray far above or below the annual average of 25° C (77° F).

When to go: All year round for whales and dolphins; December to March are usually the best months for sightings of Sperm Whales.

Getting there: Flights from Miami and Tampa (via Puerto Rico) or transfers from Antigua, Barbados, Virgin Islands, St Maarten, Guadeloupe, Martinique and St Lucia. Or there is a 300-seat catamaran ferry which operates between Guadeloupe, Dominica, Martinique and St Lucia.

Water temperature: Average 26° C (80° F) but can drop lower in the winter months. Visibility is usually around 25–30 m (80–100 ft).

Quality of marine life: Spectacular, the reefs more closely resemble those of the Pacific for quality, diversity and colour. Sperm Whales breed in the waters and sightings are common. So far 22 different types of cetaceans have been identified.

Depth of dives: Averages around 12–18 m (40–60 ft) but you will go below 30 m (100 ft) in the Danglebens crater. Whale watching is only by snorkel, which is also the best way to experience some of the reefs.

Dive practicalities: Care should be taken with exposure to the sun, particularly while travelling on the dive boats. A high-factor waterproof sunscreen should be worn at all times as well as a hat.

Left: One of the main species of fish found around the shallower sections of the RMS Rhone are Longspine Squirrelfish (Holocentrus rufus). A favourite food of grouper, they hide in coral recesses or in the wreckage during daylight hours.

British Virgin Islands: The RMS *Rhone*

Built in the UK and launched on 11 February 1865, the **RMS *Rhone*** was a royal mail steam packet ship of 2,738 gross registered tons, and measuring 95 m (310 ft) long and 12 m (40 ft) wide.

She was at anchor outside Great Harbour on Peter Island on the morning of 29 October 1867, under the command of Captain Robert F. Wooley, when the worst hurricane ever to hit the Virgin Islands descended with devastating force. The ship's anchor chain broke, causing the ship to founder on Salt Island. She split her hull and sank immediately, taking with her all on board with the exception of one passenger and 21 crew. Captain Wooley was never seen again. At least 75 other ships and more than 500 lives were lost in that tempest.

Now regarded as one of the top ten shipwrecks in the world, the RMS *Rhone* was declared a National Marine Park in 1980, the first of its kind in the British Virgin Islands.

The *Rhone* lies in two distinct parts from a depth of 6 to 27 m (20 to 90 ft) with the forward part of the hull and bowsprit in the deepest water. You are able to swim through the ribs of the ship, where there are numerous schools of snapper and squirrel fish. Encrusting corals, small sea fans and plumes adorn the upturned port side of the hull.

The stern of the ship is now completely opened up and you can swim along the entire length of the shaft to the gearbox which is now home to squirrel fish, snapper, Coral Banded Shrimps (*Stenopus hispidus*) and various encrusting and brightly coloured corals. Under the stern, next to the rudder, there are generally small schools of snapper. Grouper are dotted around all over the area and White-spotted Filefish (*Cantherhines macrocerus*) are common.

Opposite: Two large sections of rib stand upright and fairly close to the main section of the pointed bows. Favoured as a location for night dives, the wreck is absolutely covered in marine life.

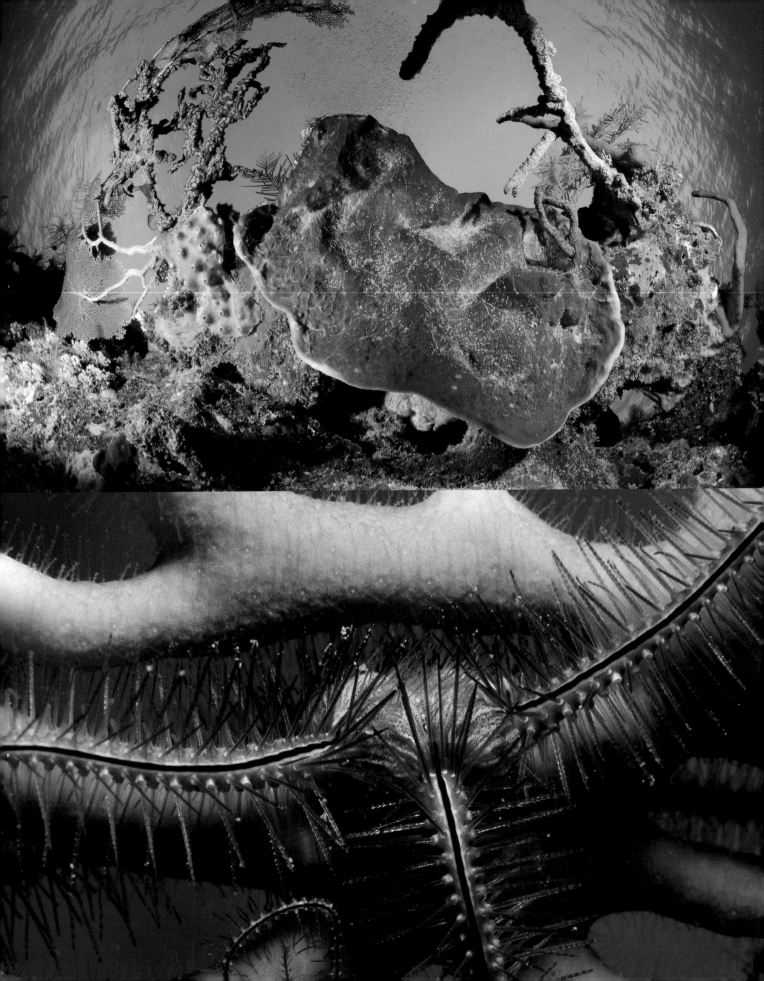

St Lucia: Anse Chastanet

Situated close to the shore on the southwest coast, just north of the region's main town Soufrière, the small designated marine park **Anse Chastanet** has so much marine life that you could spend years discovering and describing the different species. It has a shallow platform with sandy gullies between low coral spurs and a near vertical wall in some places that drops to well below the safe diving depth.

An absolutely superb night dive, as you enter the water in front of the Scuba St Lucia dive shop there are two routes which you can take. Directly out over the shallow sand patch to the start of the wall, or turn to your left and work your way along the volcanic shoreline where there is a deep cave filled with Glassy Sweepers (*Pempheris schomburgkii*) and near the entrance are small red Longlure Frogfish (*Antennarius multiocellatus*). Schools of silversides, the Caribbean equivalent of glassfish, are found just at the start of the reserve in only 3 m (10 ft) of water and they are preyed upon by needlefish and squid.

Turning right at the cave, you drop over a series of low coral ridges with sandy gullies between. On the coral spurs, which are riddled with nooks and crannies, every species of Caribbean lobster can be found wandering around in the open, particularly the slipper lobster. Red Night Shrimps (*Rhynchocinetes rigens*) are everywhere, their green reflective eyes picked out by torches. Sleeping parrotfish can be found in their cocoons, Orange-ball Anemones (*Pseudocorynactis caribbeorum*) extend their polyps and all of the daytime reef fish rest in quite open locations where they are easily approached and photographed.

Oppostie above: Curiously shaped sponges stretch out into the current underneath the Pitons, the large volcanic peaks in the southwest of the island. Sponges are the predominant form, after the soft corals.

Oppostie below: Sponge Brittle Starfish (Ophiothrix suensonii) crawl with impunity over the barbed surface of Fire Coral (Millepora alcicornis). Well-named, the harpoon-like barbs of the fire coral hook into flesh and create a strong burning sensation and a rash, similar to a burn.

Below: Sand Diver lizardfish (Synodus intermedius) perch on coral heads or hide partly submerged under soft sand – just like some lizards on land; they are waiting for small fish or crustaceans to come by. They have massive jaws lined with thousands of long teeth, almost like a net.

Dominica: Offshore Whales

Working under a special permit issued by the Ministry of Agriculture and Fisheries on Dominica to try to identify returning Sperm Whales (*Physeter macrocephalus*) and other cetaceans, divers and conservationists are given the opportunity to advance scientific study each year. Divers are allowed, under strict guidelines, to take photographic records for identification purposes: distinctive scars, coloration and missing body parts are the most obvious identifiers.

Sperm Whales are at the top of the list, as they are one of the regularly spotted species and several identified individuals have been sighted when they return over a number of years. However, any encounter with any species is always extremely welcome. As permitted divers, we were soon treated to aerobatic displays by Spinner Dolphins (*Stenella longirostris*), Bottlenose Dolphins (*Tursiops truncatus*), Pantropical Dolphins (*Stenella attenuata*), Fraser's Dolphins (*Lagenodelphis hosei*) and Spotted Dolphins (*Stenella frontalis*) riding the bow wave of our research boat. In the same dolphin super family but curiously given a 'whale' name, there were also pilot whales, False Killer Whales (*Pseudorca crassidens*) and Pygmy Sperm Whales (*Kogia breviceps*).

Above: Sperm Whales (Physeter macrocephalus) *enter Dominican waters from November through March as they migrate north from the Antarctic.*

The marine life found round this area of Dominica is regarded as second to none in the Caribbean. **Danglebens** is a site located fairly close to shore and is the inner flanks of an extinct volcano. Essentially there are a series of large pinnacles, probably better described as large coral 'bommies' which stand in a ring around the edge of the volcanic basin. There is a wide coral rubble floor at around 15 m (50 ft) between the mounds. The sides are steeply sloped on the inside, but quite vertical and dropping in layers into the crater. Depths of the pinnacles range from 12–25 m (40–80 ft) and they are covered with a superb variety of corals and sponges. Large black coral trees are found in the craters, as well as barrel sponges, tube sponges, encrusting gorgonians and crinoids. Small redband lobsters, cleaner shrimps, Honeycomb Cowfish (*Acanthostracion polygonius*), forked anemones, garden eels and Spotted Moray eels (*Gymnothorax moringa*) are absolutely everywhere. Creole Wrasse, Bar Jacks (*Carangoides ruber*) and chromis are found in the water column as you make your way back up.

Left: At least half a dozen species of true dolphins, plus many others in the family group are found in these Caribbean waters. Always riding the bow waves of boats, many different groups come together when feeding amongst the large bait balls of fish.

Below: Pods of False Killer Whales (Pseudorca crassidens) actively hunt dolphins and young whales, often driving them away from the coast where they can be picked off more easily.

Bermuda

Bermuda is a unique island ecosystem located at a high latitude (32°N, 65°W) in the North Atlantic. The warming influence of the Gulf Stream which flows around the islands moderates the air temperature and allows for the growth of hard and soft corals that are not found anywhere else as far north as this. Undoubtedly the cooler water temperatures in the winter will reduce the diversity of Caribbean species, but this may be also due to the fact that Bermuda is about 1,200 km (750 miles) from Florida and the Bahamas. But that didn't stop the lionfish from reaching her shores.

Admiral Sir George Somers was on his way to Jamestown, Virginia when his fleet of nine ships was scattered during a hurricane in 1609. His ship the *Sea Venture* was wrecked, but his crew managed to get ashore where they found a paradise where the animals were tame and unafraid of man. Somers and his crew built two small craft from the *Sea Venture*'s remains and the island's own cedar trees, and eventually managed to reach their original destination of Jamestown in Virginia. Word of Bermuda's charms soon got back to Britain, resulting in the first colonists arriving in 1612.

Bermuda was in an enviable position in the centre of the trade routes bringing every fleet of ships past her shores on their way home to Europe. Now over 400 shipwrecks, spanning several centuries, spread out over the most northerly coral reef platform on the planet.

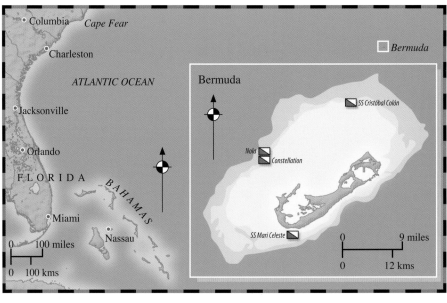

Opposite: Clockwise from top left: seen through an old porthole, a diver descends to one of the many historic shipwrecks found around this isolated seamount archipelago; Flatts Bridge is at the entrance to Harrington Sound and has a huge tidal flow making for exciting diving; 'deadeyes' are found on a few of Bermuda's historic shipwrecks, they were once pulleys for the ship's rigging; ancient sandstone mill-wheels can be found amidst the remains of the Caesar, they were used as the ship's ballast for her transatlantic crossing.

TRAVEL ADVISORY BERMUDA

Climate: The high latitude of Bermuda (32°N) makes it susceptible to the winter gales from the United States. Air temperature fluctuates strongly with the seasons, dropping to 8° C (46° F) with the passage of strong winter lows, while summer highs bring high humidity and temperatures peaking at 35° C (95° F). Rainfall averages 147 cm (58 in) and is evenly distributed throughout the year.

When to go: All-year-round, but the best times to visit are mid April to June and October to November. The prime season for diving both wrecks is August through October, when visibility is usually at its best and the water temperature is still high.

Getting there: International flights are easy into Bermuda from all of the major carriers including British Airways from London and American Airlines from several United States hub airports. The airport is in the north of the small archipelago in St Georges and as the speed limit is only 32 km (20 mph), it takes ages to get anywhere.

Water temperature: Range from 17–26° C (63–79° F). Bermudian waters are the clearest in the western Atlantic with 21 m (70 ft) underwater visibility being poor and 60–100 m (200–330ft) underwater visibility the norm on the outer reefs.

Quality of marine life: Bermuda has the most northerly coral reefs in the world and they abound with a wide variety of soft and hard corals, though few with any brilliant colours. Fish life is still low, but recovering after fishpots were banned by the Government.

Depth of dives: Averages around 12–18 m (40–60 ft) but there are a few very deep dives off the submarine mountain peaks to the south of the archipelago.

Dive practicalities: Care should be taken with exposure to the sun, particularly while travelling on the dive boats, as many of the wreck sites are found on the outer reefs and it may take over an hour to reach them. Pack travel-calm tablets as the sea can be choppy far offshore. During the wintertime, you need to bring your own scuba diving gear as many of the diving shops in Bermuda are closed, but they will supply tanks and air for those who wish to sample the superb shore diving around Flatts Bridge at Harrington Sound.

The *Constellation*/The *Nola*

The *Constellation* was a four-masted schooner of around 60 m (197 ft) length. She was en route to Venezuela from New York when she struck the reef around 13 km (8 miles) northwest of the Naval Dockyard in 1943. The vessel quickly sank in 9 m (30 ft) of water right next to a much older confederate ship, the *Nola* (*Montana*).

Originally built in 1918, she was pressed into service during the Second World War and was carrying a mixed inventory of thousands of bags of cement, 700 cases of Scotch whisky, sheets of plate glass, slate, yo-yos, tennis rackets, lead crucifixes, coffee cups, ceramic tiles, thousands of bottles, barrels of cold cream and 400,000 drug ampoules which included adrenaline, anti-tetanus serum, opium, morphine and penicillin.

Above: The nearby Nola, *often referred to as the* Montana, *is incredibly scenic and can be visited at the same time as the* Constellation.

Opposite: My great friend, Alan Marquardt, displays some of the drug ampoules recovered from the Constellation. *These are what inspired Peter Benchley to write his novel* The Deep.

Declared a total loss, the American Navy turned up and managed to salvage all of the whisky! In the cracks and holes that formed in the hardened cement bags, many juvenile Coneys (*Cephalopholis fulva*), speckled eels and octopuses now live. The ever-present Bermuda Chub (*Kyphosus sectatrix*) flock in hundreds here too. Algae grow very well on the cement sacks, attracting large populations of parrotfish and wrasse.

The reefs where she struck, in the vicinity of the Western Blue Cut, are renowned for their treacherous nature and in fact the *Constellation* sank only 15 m (50 ft) away from another, much older ship – originally thought to be the *Montana* (now known to be the *Nola*). The *Nola* was an American Civil War blockade runner – a 72-m (236-ft) long paddlewheel steamer – which was destroyed in 1863 under very similar conditions to those that accounted for the *Constellation*. Now she lies in three pieces. Both wrecks can be visited on a single dive. The *Constellation* is easily found as she is marked by the huge mound of cement bags, now turned to stone. All around are thousands of broken bottles including – if you are very lucky – some of the fabled drug ampoules.

Above: The Paddlewheel of the Nola is particularly obvious, completely covered in soft and hard corals.

The SS *Cristóbal Colón*

The **SS *Cristóbal Colón*** is Bermuda's largest shipwreck. She measured 152 m (499 ft) in length and was three decks high. This Spanish transatlantic luxury liner was wrecked in 1936 when Captain Crescencia Delgado mistook the navigation markers between North Rock and North Breaker. She now lies in 9–17 m (30–56 ft) of water with the wreckage spread over 300 sq m (3,230 sq ft) of seabed. She sat high and dry for some time, allowing extensive 'salvage' (read piracy) to take place. There are few homes in Bermuda that do not have 'souvenirs' from the *Cristóbal Colón*. She was eventually cleared during the Second World War when she was used for bombing practice.

Underwater, she is just a mass of twisted metal sheets. Divers can explore her machinery – the eight boilers, two propeller shafts, gearboxes and winches are the most obviously recognizable parts. Split into two main sections by a large coral head, she is completely covered in small sea fans and soft corals, small brain corals, fire coral and hydroids. Parrotfish, wrasse and tangs are found around her. This is a huge ship to explore and several dives are recommended.

The *Mari Celeste*

The *Mari Celeste*, located close to shore off the southernmost point of Bermuda, was a Confederate blockade-runner used to smuggle guns, ammunition, supplies and food to the troops of the South during the American Civil War. This side-mounted twin-paddle steamer was 68.5 m (225 ft) long. She sank quickly in 1864 after striking a reef close to shore. The wreck lies in 17 m (55 ft) of water, with one of her 4.5-m (15-ft) diameter paddlewheel frames standing upright like a miniature Ferris wheel. Very little can be found now as the sandy seabed gradually engulfs her rusting remains, now encrusted with soft and hard corals. Large lionfish can be found around her, but, as a consequence, few other small fish. While she cannot compare to the great historic shipwrecks, her history is interesting and well worth exploration.

Below: Tarpon actively hunt in the shallow grottos and swim-throughs for the schools of silverside minnows which collect from June to September.

Resources

Further Reading

Coral Sea Reef Guide, Bob Halstead, Sea
    Challengers
Coral Seas, Roger Steene, New Holland
    Publishers
Dive Atlas of the World, (editor) Jack Jackson,
    New Holland Publishers
Dive Guide Bahamas, Lawson Wood, New
    Holland Publishers
Dive Guide Cayman Islands, Lawson Wood,
    New Holland Publishers
Dive Guide Virgin Islands, Lawson Wood,
    New Holland Publishers
Dive Guide Yucatan & Cozumel, Lawson
    Wood, New Holland Publishers
Diving & Snorkelling Guide to Bermuda,
    Lawson Wood, Lonely Planet
Diving & Snorkelling Guide to Thailand,
    Frank Schneider,
    John Beaufoy Publishing
Diving & Snorkelling Guide to the Seychelles,
    Lawson Wood, Pisces Books
*Diving & Snorkelling Guide to Trinidad &
    Tobago*, Lawson Wood, Lonely Planet
*Diving & Snorkelling Guide to Tropical Marine
    Life of the Indo-Pacific Region*, Matthias
    Bergbauer and Manuela Kirschner,
    John Beaufoy Publishing
Red Sea Reef Guide, Helmut Debelius, IKAN
    Publications
*Reef Fishes, Corals & Invertebrates of the
    Caribbean*, Lawson Wood &
    Dr Elizabeth Wood, New Holland
    Publishers
Shipwrecks of the Cayman Islands, Lawson
    Wood, Aquapress
The Guide to Underwater Photography, Lawson
    Wood, Aquapress
Top Dive Sites of the Caribbean, Lawson
    Wood, New Holland Publishers
Top Dive Sites of the Indian Ocean, (editor)
    Jack Jackson, New Holland Publishers
Whalesharks, Dr David Rowat, Marine
    Conservation Society, Seychelles
World Atlas of Coral Reefs, Mark Spalding,
    Corinna Ravilious & Edmund Green,
    University of California Press

Dive Training Organizations

British Sub-Aqua Club BSAC
    www.bsac.com
Confédération Mondiale des Activités
    Subaquatiques CMAS www.cmas.org
Handicap Scuba Association HAS
    www.hsascuba.com
International Association for Handicapped
    Divers IAHD www.iahd.org
International Association of Nitrox and
    Technical Divers IANTD
    www.iantd.com
National Association of Underwater
    Instructors NAUI www.naui.org
Professional Association of Diving
    Instructors PADI International
    www.padi.com
Russian Underwater Federation RUF
    www.ruf.ru
Scottish Sub-Aqua Club SSAC
    www.scotsac.com
Scuba Schools International SSI
    www.ssiusa.com
Sub-Aqua Association SAA www.saa.org.uk
Technical Diving International TDI
    www.tdisdi.com

Other Related Organizations

British Society of Underwater Photographers
    BSoUP www.bsoup.org
Dive Assure www.diveassure.com
Divers Alert Network DAN
    www.diversalertnetwork.org
Fish Fight www.fishfight.net
Marine Conservation Society MCS
    www.mcs.org
Reef Environmental Education Foundation
    REEF www.reef.org
The Shark Trust www.sharktrust.org

Diving Magazines

Asian Diver www.asiandiver.com
Dive www.divemagazine.co.uk
Dive The World Magazine
    www.dtwmagazine.com
Diver Magazine www.divermag.com
Il Subaqueo www.subaqueo.it
Marine Diving www.marinediving.com
Scottish Diver Magazine www.scotsac.com
Scuba Diving www.scubadiving.com
Sport Diver Magazine www.sportdiver.co.uk
Sport Diver USA www.sportdiver.com
The Big Blue Magazine
    www.thebigbluemagazine.com
Unterwasser www.unterwasser.de
Wreck Diving Magazine
    www.wreckdivingmag.com

Web-based Diving and Photographic Information

www.africandiver.com
www.camerasunderwater.co.uk
www.cyberdiver.net
www.digideep.com
www.divephotoguide.com
www.divernet.com
www.divetheblue.net
www.diveweb.com
www.dpreview.com
www.exploreuw.com
www.lawsonwood.com
www.oceanleisurecameras.com
www.oceans-society.org
www.oceanvisions.co.uk
www.sea-sea.net
www.seafocus.com
www.undercurrent.org
www.underwaterjournal.com
www.underwaterphotography.com
www.underwaterphotographyguide.com
www.underwatertimes.com
www.uwpmag.com
www.uwvisions.com
www.wetpixel.com
www.xray-mag.com

Dive Travel Companies

Aggressor Fleet Liveaboards
    www.aggressor.com
Blue O Two Liveaboards
    www.blueotwo.com
Dancer Fleet Liveaboards
    www.dancerfleet.com
Dive The World www.dive-the-world.com
Dive Worldwide www.diveworldwide.com
Euro Divers www.euro-divers.com
Holiday Designers
    www.holiday-designers.co.uk
Red Sea Diving College
    www.redseacollege.com
Reef & Rainforest www.reefrainforest.com
Regal Dive www.regaldive.co.uk
Scuba Travel www.scubatravel.com
Snooba Travel www.snoobatravel.com
Sportif Dive www.sportifdive.co.uk
Werner Lau www.wernerlau.net
Worldwide Dive & Sail
    www.worldwidediveandsail.com

Index

This edition published in the United Kingdom in 2019 by John Beaufoy Publishing,
11 Blenheim Court, 316 Woodstock Road, Oxford OX2 7NS, England
www.johnbeaufoy.com
Previously published under the title *The World's Best Tropical Dive Desinations*

10 9 8 7 6 5 4 3 2 1

ISBN 978-1-912081-08-0

Edited, designed and typeset by Stonecastle Graphics
Cartography by William Smuts
Project management by Rosemary Wilkinson

Printed and bound in Malaysia by Times Offset (M) Sdn. Bhd.

Photo credits

All photographs copyright © Lawson Wood except the following:

© Gavin Anderson: 27 (top right); 29; 104; 107; 108

© Tony Backhurst: 95 (top right, bottom); 96; 102; 103

© Brandon Cole: 73 (top centre, top right); 75; 78; 81 (bottom);
    87; 92; 135 (all); 136; 138; 139; 149 (bottom); 151(top)

© Maldives Tourism Board/Ahmed Shareef Nafees: 39 (top centre)

© Maldives Tourism Board/George Fisher: 39 (top right)

© Stuart Philpot 155 (top centre, top right)

© Beccy Simnett: 63 (top right)

© David & Liz Skinner 35 (top right); 36; 37

© Gregory Sweeney: 51 (top centre); 109; 117

© Tahiti Tourism: 127 (top centre, bottom)

Author acknowledgements

There are many individuals, tourism offices, resorts and companies
whom I called on for help in this book; all of them are important
and if I have forgotten anyone's name, I apologise. It is my oversight,
not because I am ignoring you or that I am ungrateful. I would like
to thank my wife Lesley who knows what I need without me asking!
Brandon Cole, Dave and Liz Skinner, Stuart Philpot, Dr David
Rowat, Beccy Simnett, Gregory Sweeney, Gavin Anderson, Mark
Evans of Sport Diver Magazine, Nicola Greifeld of Snooba Travel,
Tony Backhurst of Scuba Travel and Dan Lion of Holiday Designers
all provided additional photographs and information for which
I am extremely grateful. I would also like to thank them for their
kindness, advice and professionalism when I shouted 'Help!' Thanks
also to Janice Mendoza (and for the liquid refreshments!), Paul
Duxfield, Bob Halstead, Ned DeLoach, Paul Humann, Nancy and
Jay Easterbrook, Mick Mayer, Sean Robinson, Arun (Izzy) Madisetti,
Gangga Divers, Eco Divers, Red Sea Diving College and the VIP
ONE, Emperor Divers, Seychelles Underwater Centre, Tahiti Tourist
Board, Bahamas Tourism Association and the Cayman Islands
Department of Tourism for their continual support. For specialist
diving equipment supply, I would like to thank Sea & Sea, Scubapro,
Stahlsac, Bob Evans of Force Fins and Niterider Dive Lights.

INDIAN OCEAN / INDO-PACIFIC

500 miles

1000 kilometres

0   500

0   1000 kilometres

Thailand
1 Richelieu Rock
Koh Surin
2 Koh Chi
3 Tranquil Bay
4 Koh Pachumba
5 Koh Torinla
The Similans
6 Three Arches
7 Christmas Point
8 Campbell's Bay
Koh Phi Phi
9 Maya Bay
10 Hin Bida
11 Koh Bida Nok
12 Koh Phi Phi
13 Losamah Bay
14 Koh Kraden
15 Rok Islands
16 Hin Mouang
17 Hin Daeng

Malaysia
Pulau Redang
1 Turtle Bay
2 Teluk Dalam
3 Tanjung Gua Kawah
4 Big Mount
5 Mini Seamount
6 Northeast Corner
Pulau Tioman
7 Northeast Corner
8 Southeast Side
9 Magicienne Rock
10 Malang Rocks
11 Pulau Tualai
12 Golden Reef
13 Pulau Labas
14 Pulau Renggis
Layang Layang
15 The Valley
16 Shark's Cave

17 Gorgonian Forest
18 D'Wall
Pulau Kapalai
19 Cleaning Station
Mabul
20 Crocodile Avenue
21 Coral Reef Garden
22 Nudibranch Centre
Sipidan
23 Barracuda Point
24 Coral Gardens
25 White Tip Avenue
26 West Ridge
27 Hanging Gardens
28 Lobster Lairs
29 Staghorn Crest
30 Mid Reef
31 Turtle Patch
32 South Point

18 Pulau Pomana Besar
19 Pulau Besar
20 Pulau Babi
21 Gosong Bone Atoll
22 Wailiti Reef
23 Maumere
24 Sebayur Besar
25 Tatawa Kecil
26 Sabolan Besar
27 Sabolan Kecil
Sulawesi
28 Efratha
29 Gangga Island
30 Lihaga
31 Paradise
32 Bangka
33 Police Pier
34 Hairball
35 Jahir
Pulau Raja Ampat
36 Waigeo
37 Batanta
38 Salawati
39 Misool
40 Verena's Garden

Indonesia
Pulau Sangakali
1 Pulau Derawan
2 Pulau Kakaban
3 Pulau Maratua
4 Manta Parade
5 Manta Avenue
6 Cuttlefish Bay
7 Turtle Town
8 Coral Gardens
9 Turtle Patch
10 Sandy Ridge
Lombok
11 Takat Malang
12 Andy's Reef
13 Simon's Reef
14 Gili Air Wall
15 Jammin Reef
Bali
16 Liberty Wreck
Flores
17 Pulau Pomana

Western Australia
1 North West Ridge
2 Turtle Mound
3 Cod Spot
4 Navy Pier
5 Ningaloo Reef

The Philippines
1 Apo Island Marine Sanctuary
2 Seiun Maru
3 Oryoku Maru
4 LST
5 El Capitan
6 The Cathedral
7 Kirby's Rock
8 Sepok Wall
9 Maint Point
10 Hole in the Wall
11 The Canyons
12 Shark Cave
13 Yapak
14 Friday's Rock
15 Crocodile Island
16 Olympia Maru
17 Irako
18 Gayangan Lake
19 Coron Bay

PHILIPPINE SEA
PHILIPPINES
PALAU
Luzon
Manila
Iloilo
Tacloban
Mindanao
Davao
Sandakan
SULU SEA
CELEBES SEA
Sulawesi
Palu
Halmahera
Sorong
Javapura
Gulf of Carpentaria
CERAM SEA
Seram
BANDA SEA
ARAFURA SEA
EAST TIMOR
Kupang
Flores
Sumba
TIMOR SEA
Darwin
Derby
Alice Springs
AUSTRALIA
WESTERN AUSTRALIA
Port Headland
Carnarvon
Perth
INDIAN OCEAN
Hainan
SOUTH CHINA SEA
Da Nang
VIETNAM
Ho Chi Minh
Palawan
BRUNEI
Borneo
MALAYSIA
SINGAPORE
Pontianak
INDONESIA
FLORES SEA
JAVA SEA
Java
Surabaya
Jakarta
Bali
Padang
Sumatra
Strait of Malacca
Gulf of Thailand
THAILAND
Bangkok
CAMBODIA
ANDAMAN SEA